tell
me
the
truth
about
life

A NATIONAL POETRY DAY
ANTHOLOGY

100 Poems That Matter

CURATED BY

CERYS MATTHEWS

All royalties from the sale of this book (a minimum of £4,000) will
be donated to the Forward Arts Foundation, a registered charity in
England and Wales (charity number 1037939).

Michael O'Mara Books Limited

First published in Great Britain in 2019 by
Michael O'Mara Books Limited
9 Lion Yard
Tremadoc Road
London SW4 7NQ

A CIP catalogue record for this book is available from
the British Library.

Papers used by Michael O'Mara Books Limited are natural,
recyclable products made from wood grown in sustainable forests.
The manufacturing processes conform to the environmental
regulations of the country of origin.

ISBN: 978-1-78929-099-8 in hardback print format
ISBN: 978-1-78929-122-3 in ebook format

1 2 3 4 5 6 7 8 9 10
www.mombooks.com

contents

'What started as a quiet hand-grasp between the poet and each individual reader had become a linking of arms; making life more bearable, the world a slightly different place.'

CERYS MATTHEWS

introduction

Certain phrases burrow deep inside you until they're in your bones: they keep you upright when bad news hits and, like a mantra, they steady the wandering mind.

I have many – lines of Leonard Cohen, of Stevie Smith, of Yrsa Daley-Ward and John Keats – and I am not alone, as I discovered when curating this anthology for National Poetry Day.

Tell Me the Truth About Life started with a call-out inviting the public to nominate poems that speak truth to them, and to say why they mattered. Truth was the key word, because it's the theme of National Poetry Day's twenty-fifth anniversary year, but apart from that I set no limit for nominations for inclusion in this crowd-sourced 'people's anthology'. The choices that flowed in astonished me in their variety, beauty and number.

Soon, friends – including singers, musicians, actors – were offering up poems that spoke truth to them; poems by Langston Hughes, by Sylvia Plath, by W. H. Auden. They were joined by friends of friends and Twitter friends – an Olympic rower, a criminologist, a nurse. Writers, artists and poets – including Michael Morpurgo, Jackie Morris, Carol Ann Duffy – responded too, often singling out poems that approached truth sideways.

The former Premier League footballer Marvin Sordell spoke up for a poem by Tony 'Longfella' Walsh that showed him a way of valuing himself that wasn't pegged to goals or salaries. Savannah Brown, a millennial with 500,000 YouTube followers, told of the struggle with teenage anxiety that lies behind the E.E. Cummings words tattooed on her arm. One politician found truth in Yeats; another tuned into the T'ang dynasty.

When Mark Gatiss nominated 'Oh Who Is That Young Sinner', a shatteringly modern A. E. Housman poem about prejudice, I realized that the original challenge had morphed into a conversation that crossed centuries as well as continents. This was no longer about poetry as 'literature'; it was about poetry and the possibilities of connection and of change.

'Rise like lions after slumber …', ''Tis better to have loved and lost/ Than never to have loved at all …', 'But westward look, the land is bright …' Yes, old chestnuts are here, but they sit alongside contemporary poems that I have come across in my own reading and listening. I did my best to shuffle them into themed chapters, but you will find shape-shifter poems that could fit into any section, including 'Good Bones', a poem by the young American Maggie Smith that took over Twitter on the day after the Orlando shooting in 2016, and then again after the murder of British MP Jo Cox in 2017.

'Good Bones' ends: 'This place could be beautiful, right?/ You could make this place beautiful.' Smith wrote those lines in a coffee shop in 2015; within a year the poem had been read by a million people, interpreted into a dance by a troupe in India, turned into a musical score for the voice and harp and translated into Spanish, Italian, French, Korean, Hindi, Tamil, Telugu and Malayalam. What started as a quiet hand-grasp between the poet and each individual reader had become a linking of arms; making life more bearable, the world a slightly different place.

CERYS MATTHEWS
London, 2019

CHAPTER 1

'an endless fountain of immortal drink': sage advice

What do people so often hope to find when they turn to poetry? Guidelines, hard-earned wisdom, eternal verities, all the things we wish we'd known 'way back then'. The poems in this opening section include several that have been tucked into the pocket of someone going on a journey, or shared at those crossroad occasions – graduations, weddings – when the 'endless fountain of immortal drink' tends to flow most generously.

Cavafy's 'Ithaka' and Max Ehrmann's much-loved 'Desiderata' are in this category, while Jack Gilbert's 'Failing and Flying' may strike a sadder note, but finds failure and pain is never just failure, nor just pain. Sound counsel, of course, is always much easier to give than to receive, so there's some terrific, ghostly advice against taking advice, too.

Piet Hein (1905–1996)

Henry Normal (producer, poet, writer) writes: Here is a handful of truth poems by Piet Hein, a Danish resistance leader who wrote short aphoristic rhymes, or 'grooks', that turned out to mean a lot more than the Nazis thought when they appeared as graffiti on walls in occupied Copenhagen.

Hein was a brilliant designer, mathematician and scientist, as well as a poet; indeed, he saw absolutely no contradiction between his callings. His grooks have a fine-tuned precision, using rhythm, rhyme, unarguable logic and the fewest possible words to deliver their wisdom.

Thoughts on a Station Platform

It ought to be plain
how little you gain
by getting excited
and vexed.

You'll always be late
for the previous train,
and always in time
for the next.

Small Things and Great

He that lets
the small things bind him
leaves the great
undone behind him.

Consolation Grook

Losing one glove
is certainly painful,
but nothing
    compared to the pain,
of losing one,
throwing away the other,
and finding
    the first one again.

The Road to Wisdom

The road to wisdom?
— Well, it's plain
and simple to express:
Err
and err
and err again
but less
and less
and less.

Kahlil Gibran (1883–1931)

The Prophet (extract)

Your joy is your sorrow unmasked …

Some of you say, 'Joy is greater than sorrow,' and others say, 'Nay, sorrow is the greater.'

But I say unto you, they are inseparable.

Together they come, and when one sits, alone with you at your board, remember that the other is asleep upon your bed.

——✦——

Naomi Shihab Nye (b. 1952)

Mary Jean Chan (poet) writes: There's something so intimate yet expansive about the way in which Naomi Shihab Nye depicts the relationship between kindness and sorrow in this poem.

Kindness

Before you know what kindness really is
you must lose things,
feel the future dissolve in a moment
like salt in a weakened broth.
What you held in your hand,
what you counted and carefully saved,
all this must go so you know
how desolate the landscape can be
between the regions of kindness.
How you ride and ride
thinking the bus will never stop,
the passengers eating maize and chicken
will stare out the window forever.

Before you learn the tender gravity of kindness
you must travel where the Indian in a white poncho
lies dead by the side of the road.
You must see how this could be you,
how he too was someone
who journeyed through the night with plans
and the simple breath that kept him alive.

Before you know kindness as the deepest thing inside,
you must know sorrow as the other deepest thing.
You must wake up with sorrow.
You must speak to it till your voice
catches the thread of all sorrows
and you see the size of the cloth.
Then it is only kindness that makes sense anymore,
only kindness that ties your shoes
and sends you out into the day to gaze at bread,
only kindness that raises its head
from the crowd of the world to say
It is I you have been looking for,
and then goes with you everywhere
like a shadow or a friend.

— ❧ —

Constantine P. Cavafy (1863–1933)

Marina, Lady Marks (historian, writer and philanthropist) writes: This poem (translated by Edmund Keeley and Philip Sherrard) represents the journey of life: our constant learning opportunities, our achievements, good and bad moments, pain and overcoming, progress and setbacks until, finally, rich in experiences and wisdom, we arrive at our final destination, our Ithaka, fulfilled and ready.

Ithaka

As you set out for Ithaka
hope your road is a long one,
full of adventure, full of discovery.
Laistrygonians, Cyclops,
angry Poseidon – don't be afraid of them:
you'll never find things like that on your way
as long as you keep your thoughts raised high,
as long as a rare excitement
stirs your spirit and your body.
Laistrygonians, Cyclops,
wild Poseidon – you won't encounter them
unless you bring them along inside your soul,
unless your soul sets them up in front of you.

Hope your road is a long one.
May there be many summer mornings when,
with what pleasure, what joy,
you enter harbours you're seeing for the first time;

may you stop at Phoenician trading stations
to buy fine things,
mother of pearl and coral, amber and ebony,
sensual perfume of every kind –
as many sensual perfumes as you can;
and may you visit many Egyptian cities
to learn and go on learning from their scholars.

Keep Ithaka always in your mind.
Arriving there is what you're destined for.
But don't hurry the journey at all.
Better if it lasts for years,
so you're old by the time you reach the island,
wealthy with all you've gained on the way,
not expecting Ithaka to make you rich.

Ithaka gave you the marvellous journey.
Without her you wouldn't have set out.
She has nothing left to give you now.

And if you find her poor, Ithaka won't have fooled you.
Wise as you will have become, so full of experience,
you'll have understood by then what these Ithakas mean.

— ✦ —

Max Ehrmann (1872–1945)

Nicky Cox MBE (editor-in-chief, *First News*) writes: I first came across this poem at the age of fourteen and read it out at a school speaking competition. I can't remember how I did in the contest, but I can still recite much of it by heart today. It's a timeless masterclass in lessons for life.

Desiderata

Go placidly amid the noise and haste,
and remember what peace there may be in silence.
As far as possible without surrender
be on good terms with all persons.
Speak your truth quietly and clearly;
and listen to others,
even the dull and the ignorant;
they too have their story.
Avoid loud and aggressive persons,
they are vexations to the spirit.
If you compare yourself with others,
you may become vain and bitter;
for always there will be greater and lesser persons than
    yourself.
Enjoy your achievements as well as your plans.
Keep interested in your own career, however humble;
it is a real possession in the changing fortunes of time.
Exercise caution in your business affairs;
for the world is full of trickery.

But let this not blind you to what virtue there is;
many persons strive for high ideals;
and everywhere life is full of heroism.
Be yourself.
Especially, do not feign affection.
Neither be cynical about love;
for in the face of all aridity and disenchantment
it is as perennial as the grass.
Take kindly the counsel of the years,
gracefully surrendering the things of youth.
Nurture strength of spirit to shield you in sudden
    misfortune.
But do not distress yourself with dark imaginings.
Many fears are born of fatigue and loneliness.
Beyond a wholesome discipline,
be gentle with yourself.
You are a child of the universe,
no less than the trees and the stars;
you have a right to be here.
And whether or not it is clear to you,
no doubt the universe is unfolding as it should.
Therefore be at peace with God,
whatever you conceive Him to be,
and whatever your labors and aspirations,
in the noisy confusion of life keep peace with your soul.
With all its sham, drudgery, and broken dreams,
it is still a beautiful world.
Be cheerful.
Strive to be happy.

John Keats (1795–1821)

Max Richter (composer, musician) writes: This opening stanza is a kind of miracle. For me, it is one of the neatest encapsulations of the potential of creative work, and the role it can play in our ordinary lives; beauty as a tool to help us navigate our day-to-day.

Over the years I've returned to this poem many times. Keats, like his spiritual twin Schubert, knows that life is often blunt and cruel and he doesn't sugar-coat it, but he also knows that he has a secret weapon: a humane and enquiring creative mind that illuminates the world around it to our benefit, and that this act of creativity causes the world to be, if ever so slightly and only for a moment, an easier place to live.

Endymion (extract)

A thing of beauty is a joy for ever:
Its loveliness increases; it will never
Pass into nothingness; but still will keep
A bower quiet for us, and a sleep
Full of sweet dreams, and health, and quiet breathing.
Therefore, on every morrow, are we wreathing
A flowery band to bind us to the earth,
Spite of despondence, of the inhuman dearth
Of noble natures, of the gloomy days,
Of all the unhealthy and o'er-darkened ways
Made for our searching: yes, in spite of all,
Some shape of beauty moves away the pall

From our dark spirits. Such the sun, the moon,
Trees old and young, sprouting a shady boon
For simple sheep; and such are daffodils
With the green world they live in; and clear rills
That for themselves a cooling covert make
'Gainst the hot season; the mid forest brake,
Rich with a sprinkling of fair musk-rose blooms:
And such too is the grandeur of the dooms
We have imagined for the mighty dead;
All lovely tales that we have heard or read:
An endless fountain of immortal drink,
Pouring unto us from the heaven's brink.

Nor do we merely feel these essences
For one short hour; no, even as the trees
That whisper round a temple become soon
Dear as the temple's self, so does the moon,
The passion poesy, glories infinite,
Haunt us till they become a cheering light
Unto our souls, and bound to us so fast,
That, whether there be shine, or gloom o'ercast,
They always must be with us, or we die.

— ✔ —

Nâzim Hikmet (1902–1963)

Neil Astley (editor) writes: Many writers have been imprisoned for their writing or beliefs, for speaking the truth. The Turkish poet Nâzim Hikmet spent much of his life in exile or in prison, his longest period of incarceration lasting from 1938 to 1950, when he was finally freed following an international campaign for his release after being on hunger strike and at risk of death. Hikmet's poetry continued to be banned in Turkey until 1965. 'On Living' was written in prison during 1947 and 1948 when he had already been locked up for ten years and resonates with so many readers not only because of that context – and also because many writers are still imprisoned in Turkey now for speaking the truth – but primarily because the poem asserts that living a true life gives us freedom, whatever harsh conditions we are forced to endure.

On Living

I

Living is no laughing matter:
    you must live with great seriousness
        like a squirrel, for example –
  I mean without looking for something beyond and above
living,
      I mean living must be your whole occupation.
Living is no laughing matter:
    you must take it seriously,
    so much so and to such a degree
  that, for example, your hands tied behind your back,
          your back to the wall,

or else in a laboratory
   in your white coat and safety glasses,
   you can die for people –
even for people whose faces you've never seen,
even though you know living
   is the most real, the most beautiful thing.
I mean, you must take living so seriously
   that even at seventy, for example, you'll plant olive trees –
   and not for your children, either,
   but because although you fear death you don't believe it,
   because living, I mean, weighs heavier.

II

Let's say we're seriously ill, need surgery –
which is to say we might not get up
          from the white table.
Even though it's impossible not to feel sad
          about going a little too soon,
we'll still laugh at the jokes being told,
we'll look out the window to see if it's raining,
or still wait anxiously
          for the latest newscast. . .
Let's say we're at the front –
   for something worth fighting for, say.
There, in the first offensive, on that very day,
   we might fall on our face, dead.
We'll know this with a curious anger,
     but we'll still worry ourselves to death
     about the outcome of the war, which could last years.

Let's say we're in prison
and close to fifty,
and we have eighteen more years, say,
          before the iron doors will open.
We'll still live with the outside,
with its people and animals, struggle and wind –
               I mean with the outside beyond the walls.
I mean, however and wherever we are,
     we must live as if we will never die.

III

This earth will grow cold,
a star among stars
          and one of the smallest,
a gilded mote on blue velvet –
     I mean *this*, our great earth.
This earth will grow cold one day,
not like a block of ice
or a dead cloud even
but like an empty walnut it will roll along
          in pitch-black space . . .
You must grieve for this right now
– you have to feel this sorrow now –
for the world must be loved this much
               if you're going to say 'I lived'. . .

— ✦ —

Jack Gilbert (1925–2012)

Failing and Flying

Everyone forgets that Icarus also flew.
It's the same when love comes to an end,
or the marriage fails and people say
they knew it was a mistake, that everybody
said it would never work. That she was
old enough to know better. But anything
worth doing is worth doing badly.
Like being there by that summer ocean
on the other side of the island while
love was fading out of her, the stars
burning so extravagantly those nights that
anyone could tell you they would never last.
Every morning she was asleep in my bed
like a visitation, the gentleness in her
like antelope standing in the dawn mist.
Each afternoon I watched her coming back
through the hot stony field after swimming,
the sea light behind her and the huge sky
on the other side of that. Listened to her
while we ate lunch. How can they say
the marriage failed? Like the people who
came back from Provence (when it was Provence)
and said it was pretty but the food was greasy.
I believe Icarus was not failing as he fell,
but just coming to the end of his triumph.

Alfred, Lord Tennyson (1809–1892)

In Memoriam A. H. H. OBIIT MDCCCXXXIII: 27

I envy not in any moods
    The captive void of noble rage,
    The linnet born within the cage,
That never knew the summer woods:

I envy not the beast that takes
    His license in the field of time,
    Unfetter'd by the sense of crime,
To whom a conscience never wakes;

Nor, what may count itself as blest,
    The heart that never plighted troth
    But stagnates in the weeds of sloth;
Nor any want-begotten rest.

I hold it true, whate'er befall;
    I feel it, when I sorrow most;
    'Tis better to have loved and lost
Than never to have loved at all.

— ✦ —

Eunice de Souza (b. 1940)

Advice to Women

Keep cats
if you want to learn to cope with
the otherness of lovers.
Otherness is not always neglect –
Cats return to their litter trays
when they need to.
Don't cuss out of the window
at their enemies.
That stare of perpetual surprise
in those great green eyes
will teach you
to die alone.

———✦———

A.S.J. Tessimond (1902–1962)

Sarah Hosking (charity director) writes: I first heard this on *Poetry Please*. I looked up Tessimond at the Poetry Library; a good poet, modest and unassuming, he died in mid-life.

It should be a despairing poem, the dead trying (as in many a Bible story, the rich man and the pauper) to tell the living to live better. But at least the ghost is trying to get us to mend our ways and its sweet language somehow cleans the message.

Whisper of a Thin Ghost

I bought the books of the Careful-Wise
And I read the rules in a room apart
And I learned to clothe my flinching heart
Against hate and love and inquisitive eyes
In the Coat of Caution, the Shirt of Pride.
And then, the day before I died,
I found that the rules of the wise had lied:
That life was a blood-warm stream that ran
Through the fields of death, and that no man can
Bathe in the stream but the naked man.
And that is why my ghost now must
So grope, so grieve, as grieve all those
In whom death found no wounds to close,
In whom dust found no more than dust.

CHAPTER 2

'tell all the truth but tell it slant': different ways of looking

Poets make things up. Poems aren't truth, though they may enable glimpses of truth, or school us in new ways of recognizing it. This makes the poems in this section so intriguing, because from Kubla Khan's pleasure dome to Larkin's 'An Arundel Tomb', they teem with visions, exaggerations, uncertainties, lies, contradictions, idealism and every flavour of fable and evasion.

Emily Dickinson imagines Truth as a blinding dazzle, too huge to be grasped except perhaps in the gaps between her words.

Naturally, there is a unicorn in this chapter.

Emily Dickinson (1830–1886)

Nikita Gill (writer and poet) writes: When I was little, my mother didn't sing me lullabies. Instead she told me what we called *baats* – poetic reminiscences of her earliest memories, stories passed down from her mother, and her mother's mother. They were short, succinct, filled with lessons and wisdom, mixed with Punjabi and Kashmiri folklore and folk songs, as well as the politics and battles of the area. There, in the Delhi monsoons, with a cup of tea in my hand and Mama's stories in my ear, I learned what a deeply emotional and personal thing poetry was.

Growing up, reading was what I turned to in times of crisis. Poetry changed me as a human being. I considered the words of Emily Dickinson sacred – 'Tell all the truth but tell it slant' – while Sylvia Plath was able to articulate feelings that felt too big to fit in my child's body. Maya Angelou later validated my experience as a young woman of colour. The fact that these women were writing to us from dozens of years away transformed books into time-travelling devices. And I began to realize how much of the trajectory of my life was tied to words, and to poetry.

Tell all the truth but tell it slant

Tell all the truth but tell it slant –
Success in Circuit lies
Too bright for our infirm Delight
The Truth's superb surprise
As Lightning to the Children eased
With explanation kind
The Truth must dazzle gradually
Or every man be blind –

The Soul's distinct connection

The Soul's distinct connection
With immortality
Is best disclosed by Danger
Or quick Calamity –

As Lightning on a Landscape
Exhibits Sheets of Place –
Not yet suspected – but for Flash –
And Click – and Suddenness.

I dwell in Possibility

I dwell in Possibility –
A fairer House than Prose –
More numerous of Windows –
Superior – for Doors –

Of Chambers as the Cedars –
Impregnable of Eye –
And for an Everlasting Roof
The Gambrels of the Sky –

Of Visitors – the fairest –
For Occupation – This –
The spreading wide my narrow Hands
To gather Paradise –

—— ❥ ——

Samuel Taylor Coleridge (1772–1834)

Jonathan Douglas (director, National Literacy Trust, former librarian) writes: I have no memory of learning 'Kubla Khan' by heart but for as long as I can remember I've known every word by heart. It's the product of genius and shedloads of opium. It's the closest words get to turning into music. At its heart is the poet himself, his creativity turning him into a supernatural being with flashing eyes and floating hair. This is the power of the poetic genius. I've been privileged to meet many poets and I can honestly say I've seen this spark many times, even when its hidden behind a pair of specs and under well-kempt hair.

Kubla Khan

Or, a vision in a dream. A Fragment.

In Xanadu did Kubla Khan
A stately pleasure-dome decree:
Where Alph, the sacred river, ran
Through caverns measureless to man
   Down to a sunless sea.
So twice five miles of fertile ground
With walls and towers were girdled round;
And there were gardens bright with sinuous rills,
Where blossomed many an incense-bearing tree;
And here were forests ancient as the hills,
Enfolding sunny spots of greenery.

But oh! that deep romantic chasm which slanted
Down the green hill athwart a cedarn cover!
A savage place! as holy and enchanted
As e'er beneath a waning moon was haunted
By woman wailing for her demon-lover!
And from this chasm, with ceaseless turmoil seething,
As if this earth in fast thick pants were breathing,
A mighty fountain momently was forced:
Amid whose swift half-intermitted burst
Huge fragments vaulted like rebounding hail,
Or chaffy grain beneath the thresher's flail:
And mid these dancing rocks at once and ever
It flung up momently the sacred river.
Five miles meandering with a mazy motion

Through wood and dale the sacred river ran,
Then reached the caverns measureless to man,
And sank in tumult to a lifeless ocean;
And 'mid this tumult Kubla heard from far
Ancestral voices prophesying war!
 The shadow of the dome of pleasure
 Floated midway on the waves;
 Where was heard the mingled measure
 From the fountain and the caves.
It was a miracle of rare device,
A sunny pleasure-dome with caves of ice!

 A damsel with a dulcimer
 In a vision once I saw:
 It was an Abyssinian maid
 And on her dulcimer she played,
 Singing of Mount Abora.
 Could I revive within me
 Her symphony and song,
 To such a deep delight 'twould win me,
That with music loud and long,
I would build that dome in air,
That sunny dome! those caves of ice!
And all who heard should see them there,
And all should cry, Beware! Beware!
His flashing eyes, his floating hair!
Weave a circle round him thrice,
And close your eyes with holy dread
For he on honey-dew hath fed,
And drunk the milk of Paradise.

Mary Jean Chan (b. 1990)

Leaf Arbuthnot (journalist) writes: Mary Jean Chan is a young London poet born in Hong Kong. She grew up speaking Cantonese as well as English.

'//' is about sexuality and family, belonging and home, intergenerational chafing.

'I have stopped believing that secrets are a beautiful way // to die.' The words ring with the authority of one who has laboured to find the truth and now possesses it, armed even to endure impossible family gatherings: 'dinner together won't kill us all'.

//

My mother lays the table with chopsticks & ceramic
spoons, expects you to fail at dinner. To the Chinese,

you and I are chopsticks: lovers with the same anatomies.
My mother tells you that *chopsticks* in Cantonese sounds

like *the swift arrival of sons*. My mother tongue rejoices
in its dumbness before you as expletives detonate: *[two*

women] [two men] [disgrace]. Tonight, I forget I am
bilingual. I lose my voice in your mouth, kiss till blood

comes so *sorry* does not slip on an avalanche of syllables
into sorrow. I tell you that as long as we hold each other,

no apology will be enough. Tonight, I am dreaming again
of tomorrow: another chance to eat at the feast of the living

with chopsticks balanced across the bridges of our hands
as we imbibe each *yes*, spit out every *no* among scraps of

shell or bone. Father says: *kids these days are not as tough
as we used to be. So many suicides in one week.* How many

times have you and I wondered about leaving our bodies
behind, the way many of us have already left? My friend's

sister loved a woman for ten years and each word she says
to her mother stings like a papercut. Each word she does

not say burns like the lines she etches carefully into skin.
I have stopped believing that secrets are a beautiful way

to die. You came home with me for three hundred days –
to show my family that dinner together won't kill us all.

— ✦ —

Mirza Ghalib (1797–1869)

Adil Ray (actor) writes: Here's a poem I return to, translated into English from Urdu. Ghalib was a poet born in 1797 in Agra, at the end of the Mughal empire, still revered today. I visited his house in Delhi recently: it's more like a shrine. He's not a pious poet: he believes in the good things of life. For a Muslim to be so challenging back then goes against everything we have been brought up with.

If Your Prayers

If your prayers are potent, Mullah,
Move this mosque my way.

Or have a drink or two with me,
And we'll see the minarets sway.

—— ✦ ——

Rachel Rooney (b. 1962)

David Gray (singer, songwriter) writes: This speaks truth to me as a poem because it neatly lays bare some of the complexities behind human trickery and misrepresentation. Contained within each of us is both spider and fly; we must learn to deceive others but as such, perhaps, cannot help but deceive ourselves.

The Art of Deception

Deception is an art I've come to learn.
Like webs that garden spiders carefully weave
it takes a little effort, and in turn
an unsuspecting fly that might believe.

The yarn you spin must always be secure.
The words rehearsed. If using alibis
it helps to fix them first. And do ensure
misleading truths are knotted with the lies.

The body language needs to be relaxed.
Uncross the legs, reveal an open palm.
Maintain unblinking eye-to-eye contact.
A reassuring hand upon an arm.

I know all this. Yet I identify
not with the artful spider, but the fly.

Elizabeth Bishop (1911–1979)

Imtiaz Dharker (poet, artist, film-maker) writes: This poem is a cleverly constructed lie that struggles against the truth of the last word – 'disaster'. It starts off innocently, the tone deceptively cool and light. Stanzas two and three pretend to be a set of instructions on how to master the art of losing, with situations that seem trivial and almost amusing, 'the fluster of lost door keys', 'places, and names'. Then the losses become personal, and grow to huge proportions: the mother's watch, houses, cities, rivers, a continent, all dismissed as if casually, 'it wasn't a disaster'. The last stanza comes face-to-face with the final loss, 'losing you (the joking voice…)', and the command '(*Write* it!)' that forces its way to the truth.

The poem is a villanelle, which, at its worst, can be a self-consciously 'artful' form, but here its artifice heightens the reality of 'disaster' at the end.

— ✒ —

One Art

The art of losing isn't hard to master;
so many things seem filled with the intent
to be lost that their loss is no disaster.

Lose something every day. Accept the fluster
of lost door keys, the hour badly spent.
The art of losing isn't hard to master.

Then practice losing farther, losing faster:
places, and names, and where it was you meant
to travel. None of these will bring disaster.

I lost my mother's watch. And look! my last, or
next-to-last, of three loved houses went.
The art of losing isn't hard to master.

I lost two cities, lovely ones. And, vaster,
some realms I owned, two rivers, a continent.
I miss them, but it wasn't a disaster.

—Even losing you (the joking voice, a gesture
I love) I shan't have lied. It's evident
the art of losing's not too hard to master
though it may look like (*Write* it!) like disaster.

—❧—

Czesław Milosz (1911–2004)

Incantation

Human reason is beautiful and invincible.
No bars, no barbed wire, no pulping of books,
No sentence of banishment can prevail against it.
It establishes the universal ideas in language,
And guides our hand so we write Truth and Justice
With capital letters, lie and oppression with small.
It puts what should be above things as they are,
Is an enemy of despair and a friend of hope.
It does not know Jew from Greek or slave from master,
Giving us the estate of the world to manage.
It saves austere and transparent phrases
From the filthy discord of tortured words.
It says that everything is new under the sun,
Opens the congealed fist of the past.
Beautiful and very young are Philo-Sophia
And poetry, her ally in the service of the good.
As late as yesterday Nature celebrated their birth,
The news was brought to the mountains by a unicorn and
    an echo.
Their friendship will be glorious, their time has no limit.
Their enemies have delivered themselves to destruction.

Cole Porter (1891–1964)

Always True to You, Baby (in My Fashion)

Oh, Bill,
Why can't you behave?
Why can't you behave?
How in hell can you be jealous
When you know, baby, I'm your slave?
I'm just mad for you
And I'll always be
But naturally

If a custom-tailored vet
Asks me out for something wet
When the vet begins to pet, I cry 'Hooray!'
But I'm always true to you, darlin', in my fashion.
Yes, I'm always true to you, darlin', in my way.

I enjoy a tender pass
By the boss of Boston, Mass.,
Though his pass is middle-class and not Backa Bay.
But I'm always true to you, darlin', in my fashion,
Yes, I'm always true to you, darlin', in my way.

There's a madman known as Mack
Who is planning to attack,
If his mad attack means a Cadillac, okay!
But I'm always true to to you, darlin', in my fashion,
Yes, I'm always true to you, darlin', in my way.

I've been asked to have a meal
By a big tycoon in steel,
If the meal includes a deal, accept I may.
But I'm always true to you, darlin', in my fashion,
Yes, I'm always true to you, darlin', in my way.

I could never curl my lip
To a dazzlin' diamond clip,
Though the clip meant 'Let 'er rip', I'd not say 'Nay!'
But I'm always true to to you, darlin', in my fashion,
Yes, I'm always true to you, darlin', in my way.

There's an oil man known as Tex
Who is keen to give me checks,
And his checks, I fear, mean that sex is here to stay!
But I'm always true to you, darlin', in my fashion,
Yes, I'm always true to you, darlin', in my way.

There's a wealthy Hindu priest
Who's a wolf, to say the least,
When the priest goes too far East, I also stray.
But I'm always true to to you, darlin', in my fashion,
Yes, I'm always true to you, darlin', in my way.

There's a lush from Portland, Ore.,
Who is rich but such a bore,
When the bore falls on the floor, I let him lay.
But I'm always true to to you, darlin', in my fashion,
Yes, I'm always true to you, darlin', in my way.

Mister Harris, plutocrat,
Wants to give my cheek a pat,
If the Harris pat means a Paris hat, oo-la-la!
Mais je suis toujours fidèle, darlin', in my fashion,
Oui, je suis toujours fidèle, darlin', in my way.

From Ohio, Mister Thorne
Calls me up from night 'til morn,
Mister Thorne once corner'd corn and that ain't hay.
But I'm always true to to you, darlin', in my fashion,
Yes, I'm always true to you, darlin', in my way.

From Milwaukee, Mister Fritz
Often moves me to the Ritz,
Mister Fritz is full of Schlitz and full of play.
But I'm always true to to you, darlin', in my fashion,
Yes, I'm always true to you, darlin', in my way.

Mister Gable, I mean Clark,
Wants me on his boat to park,
If the Gable boat means a sable coat, anchors aweigh!
But I'm always true to to you, darlin', in my fashion,
Yes, I'm always true to you, darlin', in my way.

— ❡ —

Brian Bilston (b. 1970)

At the Intersection

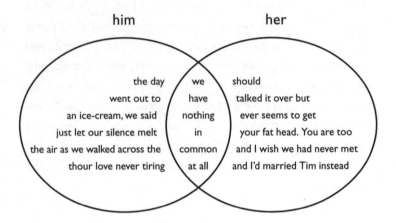

— ✦ —

Selima Hill (b. 1945)

Pascale Petit (poet) writes: Selima Hill is a truth-teller and although those truths may be uncomfortable, as in 'Why I Left You', which evokes a violent relationship, the poem goes beyond that particular circumstance. It is dynamic and volatile, bursting with compressed power. What are we, why are people so dangerous? The aeroplanes sucked down the speaker's throat evoke a huge image such as a black hole, and this hugeness is reinforced by the later image of stars spiralling down her ears. I'm left with a feeling of terror, as well as the exhilaration of wolflike freedom and a sense of being shown a secret truth.

Why I Left You

When you had quite finished
dragging me across your bed
like a band of swaggering late-night removal men
dragging a piano
the size and shape of the United States of America
across a tent,
I left the room,
and slipped into the garden,
where I gulped down whole mouthfuls of delicious
    aeroplanes
that taxied down my throat
still wrapped in sky
with rows of naked women in their bellies
telling me to go,

and I went,
and that's why I did it,
and everything told me so –
tracks that I knew the meaning of
like the tracks of a wolf
wolf-hunters know the exact colour of
by the tracks of the tracks alone.
You get a feeling for it.
You stand in the garden at night
with blood getting crisp on your thighs
and feel the stars spiralling right down
out of the sky into your ears,
burrowing down inside your ears
like drip-fed needles
saying *Get out. Now.*
By 'you' I mean me.
One of us had to:
I did.

———🍂———

William Shakespeare (1564–1616)

A Midsummer Night's Dream (extract)

The poet's eye, in fine frenzy rolling,
Doth glance from heaven to earth, from earth
    to heaven;
And as imagination bodies forth
The forms of things unknown, the poet's pen
Turns them to shapes and gives to airy nothing
A local habitation and a name.

—— ❡ ——

Wendy Cope (b. 1945)

Differences of Opinion

He tells her that the earth is flat —
He knows the facts, and that is that.
In altercations fierce and long
She tries her best to prove him wrong.
But he has learned to argue well.
He calls her arguments unsound
And often asks her not to yell.
She cannot win. He stands his ground.

The planet goes on being round.

Philip Larkin (1922–1985)

Giles Spackman (finance director) writes: I love the way this poem raises questions, withholding certainty, but still delivers a memorable finale whose emotional power speaks to the ages.

An Arundel Tomb

Side by side, their faces blurred,
The earl and countess lie in stone,
Their proper habits vaguely shown
As jointed armour, stiffened pleat,
And that faint hint of the absurd —
The little dogs under their feet.

Such plainness of the pre-baroque
Hardly involves the eye, until
It meets his left-hand gauntlet, still
Clasped empty in the other; and
One sees, with a sharp tender shock,
His hand withdrawn, holding her hand.

They would not think to lie so long.
Such faithfulness in effigy
Was just a detail friends would see:
A sculptor's sweet commissioned grace
Thrown off in helping to prolong
The Latin names around the base.

They would not guess how early in
Their supine stationary voyage
The air would change to soundless damage,
Turn the old tenantry away;
How soon succeeding eyes begin
To look, not read. Rigidly they

Persisted, linked, through lengths and breadths
Of time. Snow fell, undated. Light
Each summer thronged the glass. A bright
Litter of birdcalls strewed the same
Bone-riddled ground. And up the paths
The endless altered people came,

Washing at their identity.
Now, helpless in the hollow of
An unarmorial age, a trough
Of smoke in slow suspended skeins
Above their scrap of history,
Only an attitude remains:

Time has transfigured them into
Untruth. The stone fidelity
They hardly meant has come to be
Their final blazon, and to prove
Our almost-instinct almost true:
What will survive of us is love.

— ❧ —

CHAPTER 3

'the fight was fixed':
no punches pulled

There's a savage relish in 'Everybody Knows', the Leonard Cohen poem, a line from which gives this chapter its name. No one's going to pretend everything's just fine any more: it is not, it has never been, and it quite probably never will be.

Two of the most striking poems here are among the most recently written – Joanne Limburg's 'The Alice Case', from her 2017 collection *The Autistic Alice*, and Raymond Antrobus's mesmerizing 'Dear Hearing World' from *The Perseverance*, published in 2018. The conditions of autism and deafness, so often defined in terms of what's lacking, here hold mirrors up to the worlds that have shunned them.

The poems that follow are active acts of witness, whether calling out the corruption of the Tudor court with Sir Thomas Wyatt, or documenting the disappearance of Carrie Etter's blue butterflies. Are the speakers sorry to be delivering such terrible news? A little, perhaps, but it's the rage, not the regret, that sends energy crackling through these verses.

Leonard Cohen (1934–2016)

Tara Bergin (poet) writes: Weirdly, and perhaps not helpfully, my first thought on being asked about truth and poetry was a song by Leonard Cohen, 'Everybody Knows'. You may hate it ... It's best heard sung by him, I think, but even reading it on the page makes me feel delighted by its awful truth.

Everybody Knows

Everybody knows that the dice are loaded
Everybody rolls with their fingers crossed
Everybody knows the war is over
Everybody knows the good guys lost
Everybody knows the fight was fixed
The poor stay poor, the rich get rich
That's how it goes
Everybody knows

Everybody knows that the boat is leaking
Everybody knows that the captain lied
Everybody got this broken feeling
Like their father or their dog just died
Everybody talking to their pockets
Everybody wants a box of chocolates
And a long-stem rose
Everybody knows

Everybody knows that you love me baby
Everybody knows that you really do
Everybody knows that you've been faithful
Ah, give or take a night or two
Everybody knows you've been discreet
But there were so many people you just had to meet
Without your clothes
And everybody knows

Everybody knows, everybody knows
That's how it goes
Everybody knows

Everybody knows, everybody knows
That's how it goes
Everybody knows

And everybody knows that it's now or never
Everybody knows that it's me or you
And everybody knows that you live forever
Ah, when you've done a line or two
Everybody knows the deal is rotten
Old Black Joe's still pickin' cotton
For your ribbons and bows
And everybody knows

And everybody knows that the Plague is coming
Everybody knows that it's moving fast
Everybody knows that the naked man and woman
Are just a shining artifact of the past
Everybody knows the scene is dead
But there's gonna be a meter on your bed
That will disclose
What everybody knows

And everybody knows that you're in trouble
Everybody knows what you've been through
From the bloody cross on top of Calvary
To the beach of Malibu
Everybody knows it's coming apart
Take one last look at this Sacred Heart
Before it blows
And everybody knows

Everybody knows, everybody knows
That's how it goes
Everybody knows

Everybody knows, everybody knows
That's how it goes
Everybody knows

Everybody knows, everybody knows
That's how it goes
Everybody knows

Everybody knows

A. E. Housman (1859–1936)

Mark Gatiss (actor, writer) writes: I've chosen 'Oh Who Is That Young Sinner' by A. E. Housman. It's a very beautiful and powerful poem inspired by a real incident, when Oscar Wilde was briefly at Clapham Junction station, being transferred to Reading Gaol. He was recognized and spat at by the mob, and Housman puts us in the position of an observer. But one with (perhaps shame-faced?) sympathy for the victim.

What he articulates brilliantly is that the 'young sinner' has not made a choice but that his nature is as much a part of him as the colour of his hair. That though society has made him 'hide' they've now 'pulled the beggar's hat off for the world to see and stare'. There's proper rage, too, in those closing lines. It's a wonderful poem.

Oh Who Is That Young Sinner

Oh who is that young sinner with the handcuffs on his
    wrists?
And what has he been after that they groan and shake their
    fists?
And wherefore is he wearing such a conscience-stricken air?
Oh they're taking him to prison for the colour of his hair.

'Tis a shame to human nature, such a head of hair as his;
In the good old time 'twas hanging for the colour that it is;
Though hanging isn't bad enough and flaying would be fair
For the nameless and abominable colour of his hair.

Oh a deal of pains he's taken and a pretty price he's paid
To hide his poll or dye it of a mentionable shade;
But they've pulled the beggar's hat off for the world to see
and stare,
And they're haling him to justice for the colour of his hair.

Now 'tis oakum for his fingers and the treadmill for his feet
And the quarry-gang on Portland in the cold and in the
heat,
And between his spells of labour in the time he has to spare
He can curse the God that made him for the colour of his
hair.

— ✦ —

Joanne Limburg (b. 1970)

Steve Silberman (author, academic) writes: 'The Alice Case' is a brilliant representation of the surreal predicament that autistic adults like Limburg find themselves in when their identities are reduced to mere checklists of deficits and dysfunctions by the medical establishment. I love how Limburg uses the line breaks to intensify the feeling of Alice being under relentless assault, cloaked in the condescending language of diagnosis, and particularly admire the way that Alice herself suddenly and awkwardly appears in a conversation *about her*, which parallels the emergence of the adult autistic community in the 1990s, when they began demanding representation in the public conversation about autism.

The Alice Case

'The problem with Alice', the Caterpillar says,
  'is her rigidity of thought.'

'Yes', says Humpty Dumpty,
  'and her lack of empathy.'

'Indeed', says the Caterpillar.
  'Her mind-blindness.'

'Yes', says Humpty Dumpty.
  'Her inability to read faces.'

'Indeed', says the Caterpillar.
  'Or tone of voice.'

'And then', says Humpty Dumpty,
 'there's the flatness of her affect.'

'Alongside', says the Caterpillar,
 'the strangeness of her prosody.'

'As well as', says Humpty Dumpty,
 'her adherence to routine.'

'Not forgetting', says the Caterpillar,
 'her repetitive behaviours.'

'Or her failure', says Humpty Dumpty,
 'to understand a joke.'

'Or her lack', says the Caterpillar,
 'of any feel for metaphor.'

'Or her inability', says Humpty Dumpty,
 'to hold a proper conversation…'

'Excuse me', says Alice,
 'may I say something?'

'Of course', says the Caterpillar,
 'you may say something — '

'Yes', says Humpty Dumpty,
 'and we'll tell you why it's wrong.'

Dorothy Parker (1893–1967)

Vanessa Urquhart (bookseller) writes: Dorothy Parker's frustration, claustrophobia, acidic sarcasm and wit are all in perfect harmony in this poem. It's her lashing out against the image of a respectable female literary life in the early twentieth century and, in doing so, shouting her true feelings of rage in no uncertain terms at those who would judge her – a brave move for a well-known writer. Parker's poetry was the first inkling I had that you could be both morbid and humorous, combine style with satire and malice – and still call it art. I loved it immediately.

Song of Perfect Propriety

Oh, I should like to ride the seas,
A roaring buccaneer;
A cutlass banging at my knees,
A dirk behind my ear.
And when my captives' chains would clank
I'd howl with glee and drink,
And then fling out the quivering plank
And watch the beggars sink.

I'd like to straddle gory decks,
And dig in laden sands,
And know the feel of throbbing necks
Between my knotted hands.
Oh, I should like to strut and curse
Among my blackguard crew ...
But I am writing little verse,
As little ladies do.

Oh, I should like to dance and laugh
And pose and preen and sway,
And rip the hearts of men in half,
And toss the bits away.
I'd like to view the reeling years
Through unastonished eyes,
And dip my finger-tips in tears,
And give my smiles for sighs.

I'd stroll beyond the ancient bounds,
And tap at fastened gates,
And hear the prettiest of sounds –
The clink of shattered fates.
My slaves I'd like to bind with thongs
That cut and burn and chill…
But I am writing little songs,
As little ladies will.

—— ✐ ——

Raymond Antrobus (b. 1986)

Peter Kahn (teacher) writes: I remember when I was a teenager, my Grandma Grete started losing her hearing. She had been an extrovert with an infectious laugh, a mischievous twinkle in her eye. Over time, she started retreating from conversations and preferring one-on-one interactions. I remember a faded, vacant look in her eyes, no trace of twinkle, during a birthday celebration – an outsider, shut out at her own party. 'Take your God back, though his songs/ are beautiful, they are not loud enough,' says Raymond Antrobus in 'Dear Hearing World', and I hear the thoughts in Grandma Grete's head.

Like most of my favourite poems, 'Dear Hearing World' is both personal and universal. It is grounded in specific incidents from Raymond's experience, making the reader both hear and feel him. Antrobus writes to empower inhabitants of the non-hearing world, while challenging the rest of us to check our privilege. Our 'right' to hear is not God-given. This poem ensures deaf voices are found and heard. That their truth resonates. That I can understand my Grandma Grete better, long after she has left this Earth.

Dear Hearing World

after Danez Smith

I have left Earth in search of sounder orbits,
a solar system where the space between
a star and a planet isn't empty. I have left
a white beard of noise in my place and many
of you won't know the difference. We are
indeed the same volume, all of us eventually fade.
I have left Earth in search of an audible God.
I do not trust the sound of yours.
You would not recognise my grandmother's *Hallelujah*
if she had to sign it, you would have made her sit
on her hands and put a ruler in her mouth
as if measuring her distance from holy.
Take your God back, though his songs
are beautiful, they are not loud enough.

I want the fate of Lazarus for every deaf school
you've closed, every deaf child whose confidence
has gone to a silent grave, every BSL user
who has seen the annihilation of their language,
I want these ghosts to haunt your tongue-tied hands.

I have left Earth, I am equal parts sick of your
oh, I'm hard of hearing too, just because
you've been on an airplane or suffered head colds.
Your voice has always been the loudest sound in a room.

I call you out for refusing to acknowledge
sign language in classrooms, for assessing
deaf students on what they can't say
instead of what they can, we did not ask to be a part
of the hearing world, I can't hear my joints crack
but I can feel them. I am sick of sounding out your rules —
you tell me I breathe too loud and it's rude to make noise
when I eat, sent me to speech therapists, said I was speaking
a language of holes, I was pronouncing what I heard
but your judgment made my syllables disappear,
your magic master trick hearing world — drowning out
    the quiet,
bursting all speech bubbles in my graphic childhood,
you are glad to benefit from audio supremacy,
I tried, hearing people, I tried to love you, but you laughed
at my deaf grammar, I used commas not full stops
because everything I said kept running away,
I mulled over long paragraphs because I didn't know
what a *natural break* sounded like, ~~you erased
what could have always been poetry~~

You erased what could have always been poetry.
You taught me I was inferior to standard English
	expression —
I was a broken speaker, you were never a broken
	interpreter —
taught me my speech was dry for someone who should sound
like they're under water. It took years to talk with a
	straight spine
and mute red marks on the coursework you assigned.

Deaf voices go missing like sound in space
and I have left earth to find them.

— ✒ —

W. B. Yeats (1865–1939)

Ed Balls (broadcaster and former Labour MP) writes: Politics is in turmoil at present in Britain, America and Europe. I often think of this poem and its powerful imagery.

The Second Coming

Turning and turning in the widening gyre
The falcon cannot hear the falconer;
Things fall apart; the centre cannot hold;
Mere anarchy is loosed upon the world,
The blood-dimmed tide is loosed, and everywhere
The ceremony of innocence is drowned;
The best lack all conviction, while the worst
Are full of passionate intensity.

Surely some revelation is at hand;
Surely the Second Coming is at hand.
The Second Coming! Hardly are those words out
When a vast image out of *Spiritus Mundi*
Troubles my sight: somewhere in sands of the desert
A shape with lion body and the head of a man,
A gaze blank and pitiless as the sun,
Is moving its slow thighs, while all about it
Reel shadows of the indignant desert birds.
The darkness drops again; but now I know
That twenty centuries of stony sleep
Were vexed to nightmare by a rocking cradle,
And what rough beast, its hour come round at last,
Slouches towards Bethlehem to be born?

Kayo Chingonyi (b. 1987)

Fisherman's Song

What sadness for a fisherman
to navigate the blue
    and find among receding nets
strange, underwater blooms
    that look, at first, like bladderwrack
but from a closer view
    are clumps of matted human hair
atop an acrid soup.

And what song shall this fisherman
who loves a jaunty tune
    sing to lullaby his children
when dark shapes in their room
    make night a snarling monster
only father's voice can soothe
    and who will soothe the fisherman
who navigates the blue?

— ♪ —

Carrie Etter (b. 1969)

Karner Blue

*"... a place called Karner, where in some pine barrens, on lupines,
a little blue butterfly I have described and named ought to be
    out."*

– Vladimir Nabokov

Because it used to be more populous in Illinois.

Because its wingspan is an inch.

Because it requires blue lupine.

Because to become blue, it has to ingest the leaves of a blue
    plant.

Because its scientific name, *Lycaeides melissa samuelis*, is
    mellifluous.

Because the female is not only blue but blue and orange and
    silver and black.

Because its beauty galvanizes collectors.

Because Nabokov named it.

Because its collection is criminal.

Because it lives in black oak savannahs and pine barrens.

Because it once produced landlocked seas.

Because it has declined ninety per cent in fifteen years.

Because it is.

— ✿ —

Sharon Olds (b. 1942)

I Go Back to May 1937

I see them standing at the formal gates of their colleges,
I see my father strolling out
under the ochre sandstone arch, the
red tiles glinting like bent
plates of blood behind his head, I
see my mother with a few light books at her hip
standing at the pillar made of tiny bricks,
the wrought-iron gate still open behind her, its
sword-tips aglow in the May air,
they are about to graduate, they are about to get married,
they are kids, they are dumb, all they know is they are
innocent, they would never hurt anybody.
I want to go up to them and say Stop,
don't do it – she's the wrong woman,
he's the wrong man, you are going to do things
you cannot imagine you would ever do,
you are going to do bad things to children,
you are going to suffer in ways you have not heard of,
you are going to want to die. I want to go
up to them there in the late May sunlight and say it,
her hungry pretty face turning to me,
her pitiful beautiful untouched body,
his arrogant handsome face turning to me,
his pitiful beautiful untouched body,

but I don't do it. I want to live. I
take them up like the male and female
paper dolls and bang them together
at the hips, like chips of flint, as if to
strike sparks from them, I say
Do what you are going to do, and I will tell about it.

—— ✦ ——

Stevie Smith (1902–1971)

Not Waving but Drowning

Nobody heard him, the dead man,
But still he lay moaning:
I was much further out than you thought
And not waving but drowning.

Poor chap, he always loved larking
And now he's dead
It must have been too cold for him his heart gave way,
They said.

Oh, no no no, it was too cold always
(Still the dead one lay moaning)
I was much too far out all my life
And not waving but drowning.

W. B. Yeats (1865–1939)

Crazy Jane Talks with the Bishop

I met the Bishop on the road
And much said he and I.
'Those breasts are flat and fallen now
Those veins must soon be dry;
Live in a heavenly mansion,
Not in some foul sty.'

'Fair and foul are near of kin,
And fair needs foul,' I cried.
'My friends are gone, but that's a truth
Nor grave nor bed denied,
Learned in bodily lowliness
And in the heart's pride.

'A woman can be proud and stiff
When on love intent;
But Love has pitched his mansion in
The place of excrement;
For nothing can be sole or whole
That has not been rent.'

—— ⟋ ——

Roger McGough (b. 1937)

Chris Riddell (artist) writes: As the father of an imaginative and enquiring daughter myself, Roger's poem has always spoken to me. I love its tone of wry tenderness mixed with regret. Soon our daughters will grow up and no longer need their fathers' incredibly sage advice.

The Way Things Are

No, the candle is not crying, it cannot feel pain.
Even telescopes, like the rest of us, grow bored.
Bubblegum will not make the hair soft and shiny.
The duller the imagination, the faster the car,
I am your father and this is the way things are.

When the sky is looking the other way,
do not enter the forest. No, the wind
is not caused by the rushing of clouds.
An excuse is as good a reason as any.
A lighthouse, launched, will not go far,
I am your father and this is the way things are.

No, old people do not walk slowly
because they have plenty of time.
Gardening books when buried will not flower.
Though lightly worn, a crown may leave a scar,
I am your father and this is the way things are.

No, the red woolly hat has not been
put on the railing to keep it warm.
When one glove is missing, both are lost.
Today's craft fair is tomorrow's car boot sale.
The guitarist gently weeps, not the guitar,
I am your father and this is the way things are.

Pebbles work best without batteries.
The deckchair will fail as a unit of currency.
Even though your shadow is shortening
it does not mean you are growing smaller.
Moonbeams sadly, will not survive in a jar,
I am your father and this is the way things are.

For centuries the bullet remained quietly confident
that the gun would be invented.
A drowning surrealist will not appreciate
the concrete lifebelt.
No guarantee my last goodbye is an au revoir,
I am your father and this is the way things are.

Do not become a prison-officer unless you know
what you're letting someone else in for.
The thrill of being a shower curtain will soon pall.
No trusting hand awaits a falling star
I am your father, and I am sorry
but this is the way things are.

— ❡ —

Sir Thomas Wyatt (1503–1542)

What vaileth trouth

What vaileth trouth? or, by it, to take payne?
To stryve, by stedfastnes, for to attayne,
To be iuste, and true: and fle from dowblenes:
Sythens all alike, where rueleth craftines
Rewarded is boeth fals and plain.
Sonest he spedeth, that moost can fain;
True meanyng hert is had in disdayn.
Against deceipte and dowblenes
   What vaileth trouth?

Decyved is he by crafty trayn
That meaneth no gile and doeth remayn
Within the trapp, without redresse,
But, for to love, lo, suche a maisteres,
Whose crueltie nothing can refrayn,
   What vaileth trouth?

CHAPTER 4

'rise like lions':
ballads to mobilize

I could have filled this book with poems that cry out to be cried out – battle songs to stir the spirit, calls to arms, the words needed just before the big push. The word that keeps echoing is 'rise' – see Shelley, Maya Angelou, Charlotte Mew – and many of the most frequently nominated poems share a dramatic, almost operatic quality.

Winston Churchill famously recited Arthur Hugh Clough's words during the darkest days of the Second World War: 'But westward, look, the land is bright.' But even poems whose context can only be guessed at – the Sumerian priestess Enheduanna's hymn to Inanna, nominated by historian Amanda Foreman 4,000 years after it was first composed – charge the air with energy.

Percy Bysshe Shelley (1792–1822)

The Masque of Anarchy (extract)

LXXIX

'Stand ye calm and resolute,
Like a forest close and mute,
With folded arms and looks which are
Weapons of unvanquished war.

LXXX

'And let Panic, who outspeeds
The career of armèd steeds,
Pass, a disregarded shade,
Through your phalanx undismayed.

LXXXI

'Let the laws of your own land,
Good or ill, between ye stand,
Hand to hand, and foot to foot,
Arbiters of the dispute.

LXXXII

'The old laws of England – they
Whose reverend heads with age are grey,
Children of a wiser day;
And whose solemn voice must be
Thine own echo – Liberty!

LXXXIII

'On those who first should violate
Such sacred heralds in their state
Rest the blood that must ensue,
And it will not rest on you.

LXXXIV

'And if then the tyrants dare
Let them ride among you there,
Slash, and stab, and maim, and hew, –
What they like, that let them do.

LXXXV

'With folded arms and steady eyes,
And little fear, and less surprise,
Look upon them as they slay
Till their rage has died away.

LXXXVI

'Then they will return with shame
To the place from which they came,
And the blood thus shed will speak
In hot blushes on their cheek.

LXXXVII

'Every woman in the land
Will point at them as they stand –
They will hardly dare to greet
Their acquaintance on the street.

LXXXVIII

'And the bold, true warriors
Who have hugged Danger in wars
Will turn to those who would be free,
Ashamed of such base company.

LXXXIX

'And that slaughter to the Nation
Shall steam up like inspiration,
Eloquent, oracular;
A volcano heard afar.

XC

'And these words shall then become
Like Oppression's thundered doom
Ringing through each heart and brain,
Heard again – again – again –

XCI

'Rise like Lions after slumber
In unvanquishable number –
Shake your chains to earth like dew
Which in sleep had fallen on you –
Ye are many – they are few.'

—— ✦ ——

Langston Hughes (1902–1967)

Colin Salmon (actor) writes: Hughes never forgot who he was and where he was from. It was complex, but he loved his people and his community.

He spoke of his loneliness as a child and its remedy. 'Then it was that books began to happen to me, and I began to believe in nothing but books and the wonderful world in books – where if people suffered, they suffered in beautiful language, not in monosyllables, as we did in Kansas.'

It is no accident that he would be central to the Jazz Age and Harlem Renaissance, where people suffered in beautiful songs, beautiful fashions and beautiful music. To sing of love is a revolutionary act in times of hate. Poetry by its very nature casts a spell of hope, and the most beautiful ballad can be blown by the seemingly ugliest of men. Some choose to listen, and from there a movement begins.

Dreams

Hold fast to dreams
For if dreams die
Life is a broken-winged bird
That cannot fly.

Hold fast to dreams
For when dreams go
Life is a barren field
Frozen with snow.

Fatimah Asghar (b. 1990)

Nikesh Shukla (writer and editor of *The Good Immigrant*) writes: This is about solidarity. It moves elegantly, like a rallying call to arms, a call of solidarity, a simple nod that says: I see you and I got you. This is about the complexities of taking up space. This is me having your back. This is us. Fighting for our lives. And words are our weapons.

If They Come for Us

these are my people & I find
them on the street & shadow
through any wild all wild
my people my people
a dance of strangers in my blood
the old woman's sari dissolving to wind
bindi a new moon on her forehead
I claim her my kin & sew
the star of her to my breast
the toddler dangling from stroller
hair a fountain of dandelion seed
at the bakery I claim them too
the Sikh uncle at the airport
who apologizes for the pat
down the Muslim man who abandons
his car at the traffic light drops
to his knees at the call of the Azan
& the Muslim man who drinks
good whiskey at the start of maghrib

the lone khala at the park
pairing her kurta with crocs
my people my people I can't be lost
when I see you my compass
is brown & gold & blood
my compass a Muslim teenager
snapback & high-tops gracing
the subway platform
Mashallah I claim them all
my country is made
in my people's image
if they come for you they
come for me too in the dead
of winter a flock of
aunties step out on the sand
their dupattas turn to ocean
a colony of uncles grind their palms
& a thousand jasmines bell the air
my people I follow you like constellations
we hear glass smashing the street
& the nights opening dark
our names this country's wood
for the fire my people my people
the long years we've survived the long
years yet to come I see you map
my sky the light your lantern long
ahead & I follow I follow

—— ✦ ——

Enheduanna (2285 bc–2250 bc)

Dr Amanda Foreman (historian) writes: Before the Sumerian high priestess Enheduanna, writing was anonymous. Of course, there were hymns, lamentations, poems and other works being written, but these were mainly group efforts, or had been handed down through oral tradition. It was Enheduanna, keeper of the shrine of the goddess Inanna, who put an individual stamp and interpretation on the religious hymns that she was responsible for writing, signing the wet clay tablets on which she wrote with her personal signature. Here she is, calling on the goddess for help against her enemies, who seem to be ignoring her rights and trespassing on her territory: 'as if I had never lived there'.

It's incredibly exciting: for thousands of years the notion of the 'I' has been withheld from women. Yet here, 4,000 years ago, was a woman who had such power and status, claiming her own work, her own voice, her own truth.

The Exaltation of Inanna (extract)

Great queen of queens,
issue of a holy womb for righteous divine powers,
greater than your own mother,
wise and sage,
lady of all the foreign lands,
life-force of the teeming people:
I will recite your holy song!

True goddess fit for divine powers, your splendid utterances
    are magnificent.

Deep-hearted, good woman with a radiant heart,
I will enumerate your divine powers for you!

I, Enheduanna the *en* priestess, entered my holy *jipar* in
    your service.
I carried the ritual basket, and intoned the song of joy.
But funeral offerings were brought, as if I had never lived
    there.

I approached the light, but the light was scorching hot to me.
I approached that shade, but I was covered with a storm.
My honeyed mouth became venomous.
My ability to soothe moods vanished.

Suen, tell An about Lugalane and my fate!
May An undo it for me! As soon as you tell An about it, An
    will release me.

The woman will take the destiny away from Lugalane;
    foreign lands and flood lie at her feet.
The woman too is exalted, and can make cities tremble.
Step forward, so that she will cool her heart for me.

I, Enheduanna, will recite a prayer to you.
To you, holy Inanna,
I shall give free vent to my tears like sweet beer!

Audre Lorde (1934–1992)

Jade Anouka (actor) writes: This dense and beautiful poem is both shattering and inspiring. As a self-professed black, lesbian, mother, warrior, poet, Audre Lorde spoke up for civil rights, women's rights and gay rights. She held up the truth of what it feels like to be a marginalized people and showed how the oppressed can empower themselves by joining together and finding the collective power of their voice. It's written in the style of the Catholic prayer in which the congregation responds in unison. But rather than relying on an external, distant Christian God, the power called upon lies within ourselves and in our voice. We must speak up now for the good of the future.

A Litany for Survival

For those of us who live at the shoreline
standing upon the constant edges of decision
crucial and alone
for those of us who cannot indulge
the passing dreams of choice
who love in doorways coming and going
in the hours between dawns
looking inward and outward
at once before and after
seeking a now that can breed
futures
like bread in our children's mouths
so their dreams will not reflect
the death of ours;

For those of us
who were imprinted with fear
like a faint line in the center of our foreheads
learning to be afraid with our mother's milk
for by this weapon
this illusion of some safety to be found
the heavy-footed hoped to silence us
For all of us
this instant and this triumph
We were never meant to survive.

And when the sun rises we are afraid
it might not remain
when the sun sets we are afraid
it might not rise in the morning
when our stomachs are full we are afraid
of indigestion
when our stomachs are empty we are afraid
we may never eat again
when we are loved we are afraid
love will vanish
when we are alone we are afraid
love will never return
and when we speak we are afraid
our words will not be heard
nor welcomed
but when we are silent
we are still afraid

So it is better to speak
remembering
we were never meant to survive.

---✦---

Maya Angelou (1928–2014)

Frances Houghton (rower, three-time Olympic silver medallist) writes: I found this poem two weeks after my father died and the night we had been confirmed as selected for the Olympic Team for Rio. We had been subjected to the most brutal testing process, but we would be staying together as a team.

I remember sending this poem to the girls with the message: 'All that lies before us now is adventure and opportunity. May we face it together with the unity with which we have faced adversity, and our lives will be richer for it.'

Still I Rise

You may write me down in history
With your bitter, twisted lies,
You may trod me in the very dirt
But still, like dust, I'll rise.

Does my sassiness upset you?
Why are you beset with gloom?
'Cause I walk like I've got oil wells
Pumping in my living room.

Just like moons and like suns,
With the certainty of tides,
Just like hopes springing high,
Still I'll rise.

Did you want to see me broken?
Bowed head and lowered eyes?
Shoulders falling down like teardrops,
Weakened by my soulful cries?

Does my haughtiness offend you?
Don't you take it awful hard
'Cause I laugh like I've got gold mines
Diggin' in my own backyard.

You may shoot me with your words,
You may cut me with your eyes,
You may kill me with your hatefulness,
But still, like air, I'll rise.

Does my sexiness upset you?
Does it come as a surprise
That I dance like I've got diamonds
At the meeting of my thighs?

Out of the huts of history's shame
I rise
Up from a past that's rooted in pain
I rise
I'm a black ocean, leaping and wide,
Welling and swelling I bear in the tide.

Leaving behind nights of terror and fear
I rise
Into a daybreak that's wondrously clear
I rise
Bringing the gifts that my ancestors gave,
I am the dream and the hope of the slave.
I rise
I rise
I rise.

—————

Hafiz (1315–1390)

Berserk

Once
In a while
God cuts loose His purse strings,
Gives a big wink to my orchestra.

Hafiz
Does not require
Any more prompting than that
To let
Every instrument inside
Go
Berserk.

Arthur Hugh Clough (1819–1861)

Terrance Marshman-Edwards (administrator, Open University) writes: This poem carries a great significance for me – it encourages you to continue and carry on even in the face of seemingly unconquerable circumstances.

Say Not the Struggle Nought Availeth

Say not the struggle nought availeth,
    The labour and the wounds are vain,
The enemy faints not, nor faileth,
    And as things have been they remain.

If hopes were dupes, fears may be liars;
    It may be, in yon smoke concealed,
Your comrades chase e'en now the fliers,
    And, but for you, possess the field.

For while the tired waves, vainly breaking
    Seem here no painful inch to gain,
Far back through creeks and inlets making,
    Comes silent, flooding in, the main.

And not by eastern windows only,
    When daylight comes, comes in the light,
In front the sun climbs slow, how slowly,
    But westward, look, the land is bright.

— ❧ —

Gwendolyn Brooks (1917–2000)

Paul Robeson

That time,
we all heard it.
cool and clear,
cutting across the hot grit of the day.
The major Voice.
The adult Voice
forgoing Rolling River,
forgoing tearful tale of bale and barge
and other symptoms of an old despond.
Warning, in music-words
devout and large,
that we are each other's
harvest:
we are each other's
business:
we are each other's
magnitude and bond.

——— ✦ ———

Robert Burns (1759–1796)

A Man's A Man for A' That

Is there for honest Poverty
  That hings his head, an' a' that;
The coward slave – we pass him by,
  We dare be poor for a' that!
For a' that, an' a' that.
  Our toils obscure an' a' that,
The rank is but the guinea's stamp,
  The Man's the gowd for a' that.

What though on hamely fare we dine,
  Wear hoddin grey, an' a that;
Gie fools their silks, and knaves their wine;
  A Man's a Man for a' that:
For a' that, and a' that,
  Their tinsel show, an' a' that;
The honest man, tho' e'er sae poor,
  Is king o' men for a' that.

Ye see yon birkie, ca'd a lord,
  Wha struts, an' stares, an' a' that;
Tho' hundreds worship at his word,
  He's but a coof for a' that:
For a' that, an' a' that,
  His ribband, star, an' a' that;
The man o' independent mind
  He looks an' laughs at a' that.

A prince can mak a belted knight,
  A marquis, duke, an' a' that;
But an honest man's abon his might,
  Gude faith, he maunna fa' that!
For a' that, an' a' that,
  Their dignities an' a' that;
The pith o' sense, an' pride o' worth,
  Are higher rank than a' that.

Then let us pray that come it may,
  (As come it will for a' that,)
That Sense and Worth, o'er a' the earth,
  Shall bear the gree, an' a' that.
For a' that, an' a' that,
  It's coming yet for a' that,
That Man to Man, the world o'er,
  Shall brothers be for a' that.

— ✔ —

Charlotte Mew (1869–1928)

The Call

From our low seat beside the fire
Where we have dozed and dreamed and
watched the glow
Or raked the ashes, stopping so
We scarcely saw the sun or rain
Above, or looked much higher
Than this same quiet red or burned-out fire.
To-night we heard a call,
A rattle on the window-pane,
A voice on the sharp air,
And felt a breath stirring our hair,
A flame within us: Something swift and tall
Swept in and out and that was all.
Was it a bright or a dark angel? Who can know?
It left no mark upon the snow,
But suddenly it snapped the chain
Unbarred, flung wide the door
Which will not shut again;
And so we cannot sit here any more.

We must arise and go:
The world is cold without
And dark and hedged about
With mystery and enmity and doubt,
But we must go
Though yet we do not know
Who called, or what marks we shall leave upon the snow.

CHAPTER 5

'the peace of wild things': nature's solace

Sometimes words are not enough, or too much – they feel contaminated, stale, over-used. That's when it helps to drop out and tune in to the natural world. 'For a moment not doing, nor coming undone,' as Philip Gross's 'Severn Song' has it. Brian Patten's poem 'A blade of grass', chosen by Laura Dockrill for saying so much 'while saying hardly anything' has all the simplicity and freshness of its subject matter.

The immensely popular – and frequently nominated – American poet Wendell Berry contemplates nature as a sanctuary and spiritual retreat. And though Dannie Abse's frantic wasp and Mark Waddell's suicidal possums are far more wild than peaceful, their strangely attentive poems sharpen the senses and invite us to re-learn the business of being.

Wendell Berry (b. 1934)

Jackie Morris (artist) writes: 'When despair for the world grows in me, and I wake in the night at the least sound', I find myself turning to poets, and often to 'The Peace of Wild Things'. Here I find questions and answers, and I rest in the grace of knowing that I am not alone, and that together, perhaps, we can imagine a better world.

William Sieghart (founder of National Poetry Day and the Forward Prizes) writes: I like the way this reminds us of what really matters when we are feeling at our bleakest, and gives us a sense of the natural truths all around us to find solace in.

The Peace of Wild Things

When despair for the world grows in me
and I wake in the night at the least sound
in fear of what my life and my children's lives may be,
I go and lie down where the wood drake
rests in his beauty on the water, and the great heron feeds.
I come into the peace of wild things
who do not tax their lives with forethought
of grief. I come into the presence of still water.
And I feel above me the day-blind stars
waiting with their light. For a time
I rest in the grace of the world, and am free.

Sylvia Plath (1932–1963)

Helen Sharman (astronaut) writes: Sylvia Plath's 'Stars over the Dordogne' reminds me just what it is like watching the stars from my local park, when the Earth spins and objects on the horizon loom up to block the stars from view. I loved looking at stars from the Space Station, when I could see billions of dots of steady light coming towards me. Every time I see stars now, I think about how many there must be that we cannot see and I am filled with awe at the majesty and beauty of the universe.

Stars over the Dordogne

Stars are dropping thick as stones into the twiggy
Picket of trees whose silhouette is darker
Than the dark of the sky because it is quite starless.
The woods are a well. The stars drop silently.
They seem large, yet they drop, and no gap is visible.
Nor do they send up fires where they fall
Or any signal of distress or anxiousness.
They are eaten immediately by the pines.

Where I am at home, only the sparsest stars
Arrive at twilight, and then after some effort.
And they are wan, dulled by much traveling.
The smaller and more timid never arrive at all
But stay, sitting far out, in their own dust.
They are orphans. I cannot see them. They are lost.
But tonight they have discovered this river with no trouble;
They are scrubbed and self-assured as the great planets.

The Big Dipper is my only familiar.
I miss Orion and Cassiopeia's Chair. Maybe they are
Hanging shyly under the studded horizon
Like a child's too-simple mathematical problem.
Infinite number seems to be the issue up there.
Or else they are present, and their disguise so bright
I am overlooking them by looking too hard.
Perhaps it is the season that is not right.

And what if the sky here is no different,
And it is my eyes that have been sharpening themselves?
Such a luxury of stars would embarrass me.
The few I am used to are plain and durable;
I think they would not wish for this dressy backcloth
Or much company, or the mildness of the south.
They are too puritan and solitary for that—
When one of them falls it leaves a space,

A sense of absence in its old shining place.
And where I lie now, back to my own dark star,
I see those constellations in my head,
Unwarmed by the sweet air of this peach orchard.
There is too much ease here; these stars treat me too well.
On this hill, with its view of lit castles, each swung bell
Is accounting for its cow. I shut my eyes
And drink the small night chill like news of home.

— ✦ —

Philip Gross (b. 1952)

Severn Song

(for John Karl Gross)

The Severn was brown and the Severn was blue –
not this-then-that, not either-or,
no mixture. Two things can be true.
The hills were clouds and the mist was a shore.

The Severn was water, the water was mud
whose eddies stood and did not fill,
the kind of water that's thicker than blood.
The river was flowing, the flowing was still,

the tide-rip the sound of dry fluttering wings
with waves that did not break or fall.
We were two of the world's small particular things.
We were old, we were young, we were no age at all,

for a moment not doing, nor coming undone –
words gained, words lost, till who's to say
which was the father, which was the son,
a week, or fifty years, away.

But the water said *earth* and the water said *sky*.
We were everyone we'd ever been or would be,
every angle of light that says *You*, that says *I*,
and the sea was the river, the river the sea.

Gillian Clarke (b. 1937)

Ode to Winter

We hoard light, hunkered in holt and burrow,
in cave, *cwtsh*, den, earth, hut, lair.
Sun blinks. Trees take down their hair.
Dusk wipes horizons, seeps into the room,
the last flame of geranium in the gloom.

In the shortening day, bring in the late flowers
to crisp in a vase, beech to break into leaf,
a branch of lark. Take winter by the throat.
Feed the common birds, tits and finches,
the spotted woodpecker in his opera coat.

Let's learn to love the icy winter moon,
or moonless dark and winter constellations,
Jupiter's glow, a slow, incoming plane,
neighbourly windows, someone's flickering screen,
a lamp-lit page, drawn curtains.

Let us praise intimacy, talk and books,
music and silence, wind and rain,
the beautiful bones of trees, taste of cold air,
darkening fields, the glittering city,
that winter longing, *hiraeth*, something like prayer.

Under the stilled heartbeat of trees,
wind-snapped branches, mulch and root,
a million bluebell bulbs lie low
ready to flare in lengthening light,
after the dark, the frozen earth, the snow.

Out there, fox and buzzard, kite and crow
are clearing the ground for the myth.
On the darkest day bring in the tree,
cool and pungent as forest. Turn up the music.
Pour us a glass. Dress the house in pagan finery.

— ✦ —

Eleanor Farjeon (1881–1965)

Poetry

What is Poetry? Who knows?
Not a rose, but the scent of a rose;
Not the sky, but the light in the sky;
Not the fly, but the gleam of the fly;
Not the sea, but the sound of the sea;
Not myself, but what makes me
See, hear, and feel something that prose
Cannot: and what it is, who knows?

— ✦ —

Li Bai (AD 701–AD 762)

Rory Stewart (politician and author) writes: This is the first poem I learnt when I was a child growing up in Hong Kong. It's a poem from the eighth century by a poet from the T'ang dynasty and it means a great deal to me.

Quiet Night Thoughts

床前明月光
疑是地上霜
举头望明月
低头思故乡

I can see the moon on my floor.
I think it looks like frost.
I lift my head, look at the moon,
Drop my head, remember home.

— ✦ —

W. B. Yeats (1865–1939)

Shevaun Wilder (director, Josephine Hart Poetry Foundation) writes: I have been in London for over twenty years and, still, whenever I walk down the Strand 'on the pavements grey', imaginings and memories intermingle as this lovely, lyrical poem, with its honey bees 'in the bee-loud glade' – first heard and loved in childhood – washes over me again like 'lake water lapping'.

The truth is, the ache of yearning for the home place that the poem captures, though it intensifies my sense of the émigré experience, also often satisfies the longing in my 'deep heart's core'.

The Lake Isle of Innisfree

I will arise and go now, and go to Innisfree,
And a small cabin build there, of clay and wattles made;
Nine bean-rows will I have there, a hive for the honey-bee,
And live alone in the bee-loud glade.

And I shall have some peace there, for peace comes
    dropping slow,
Dropping from the veils of the morning to where the
    cricket sings;
There midnight's all a glimmer, and noon a purple glow,
And evening full of the linnet's wings.

I will arise and go now, for always night and day
I hear lake water lapping with low sounds by the shore;
While I stand on the roadway, or on the pavements grey,
I hear it in the deep heart's core.

Imtiaz Dharker (b. 1954)

Chaudhri Sher Mobarik Looks at the Loch

Light shakes out the dishrag sky
and scatters the water with sequins. *Look, hen!*
says my father, *Loch Lomond!* as if
it were all his doing, as if he owned it,
laird of Lomond, laird of the language.
He is proud to say *hen* and even more *loch*
with an *och* not an *ock*, to speak
proper Glaswegian like a true-born Scot,
and he makes the right sound at the back
of the throat because he can say *khush*
and *khwab* and *khamosh*, because the sounds
for happy and dream are the words that swim
In the water for him, so he says it again
Hen! Look! The loch!

———

Emily Berry (b. 1981)

Canopy

The weather was inside.

The branches trembled over the glass as if to apologise; then they thumped and they came in.

And the trees shook everything off until they were bare and clean. They held on to the ground with their long feet and leant into the gale and back again.

This was their way with the wind.

They flung us down and flailed above us with their visions and their pale tree light.

I think they were telling us to survive. That's what a leaf feels like anyway. We lay under their great awry display and they tattooed us with light.

They got inside us and made us speak; I said my first word in their language: 'canopy'.

I was crying and it felt like I was feeding. Be my mother, I said to the trees, in the language of trees, which can't be transcribed, and they shook their hair back, and they bent low with their many arms, and they looked into my eyes as only trees can look into the eyes of a person, they touched me with the rain on their fingers till I was all droplets, till I was a mist, and they said they would.

Brian Patten (b. 1946)

Laura Dockrill (poet) writes: I chose this poem because when my mum and dad were breaking up I was just a teenager. We didn't really have the words to explain how we were feeling or to describe the fear of what was going to happen to us all. My dad once read me this poem on my bed and it stuck with me. It explained and said so much while saying hardly anything at all. That's why I love poetry so much. It allows you to fill in the gaps. It speaks for those moments that are too difficult to find the words for. My dad moved out not long after. We've always connected over literature and we saw Brian Patten read a few years back and it moved us both. It speaks a lot of truth – it did to me then and does, even more, to me now.

A Blade of Grass

You ask for a poem.
I offer you a blade of grass.
You say it is not good enough.
You ask for a poem.

I say this blade of grass will do.
It has dressed itself in frost,
It is more immediate
Than any image of my making.

You say it is not a poem.
It is a blade of grass and grass
Is not quite good enough.
I offer you a blade of grass.

You are indignant.
You say it is too easy to offer grass.
It is absurd.
Anyone can offer a blade of grass.

You ask for a poem.
And so I write you a tragedy about
How a blade of grass
Becomes more and more difficult to offer,

And about how as you grow older
A blade of grass
Becomes more difficult to accept.

—— ✦ ——

Mona Arshi (b. 1970)

Dr Aisha Gill (criminologist) writes: For a number of years Mona Arshi has been using her work as a way to engage with disruptive Mother Nature and the politics of truth and justice; it is this groundbreaking approach to these issues that has drawn me to her poetry.

Arshi does not just demonstrate how our lives are littered with multivalent truths; she also demonstrates an apparent crisis of justice as a universal principle of order. I love the way in which she contrasts the selfless behaviour of the octopus with the lying behaviour of humans.

Now I Know the Truth about Octopuses
(and the Lies We Tell Our Children)

No mother could give more Jim Cosgrove, Biologist

How they fashion a pillow from their front tentacles for their lovers

The Police will come if you pull down your doll's knickers.

these adept navigators in the abyssal waters

We have nothing in common with the anxious foreigner.

… feetless, escapologists

That Helen went willingly.

these great rhapsodisers of the sea …

Everything on your plate was tenderly coaxed into
    submission…

how they love and live brightly

… yes even the lamb.

their engorged hearts pulsing (they have three)

Michael Jackson died because he ate too much butter.

standing vigil over their milky teardrop babies

The blurry defenseless bee is not worth fighting for.

forsaking food, forsaking comfort

That's hair on your body, not fur.

they live not long, unnourished

That sunlight smells of nothing.

their bodies fade...

Obedience. Obedience. Obedience.

their souls finding shelter amongst the sea-grass

——— ✦ ———

Mark Waddell (b. 1966)

Janis Gilpin (speech therapist) writes: The man in this poem could be any of us, bumbling our way through our 'busy' lives, missing what is right in front of us as we spend extraordinary amounts of time in our heads or on our phones. Take the time to look up, look out, be aware, or you might miss the sound of your own falling possum.

The sound of a falling possum

the man who struggled
with spotting the obvious
had never heard
the sound of a falling possum
before
and in its own kinda way
it was
quite beautiful
before
the impact of course

he tried to resuscitate it
pumping away
at its little heart
and kissing those
funny lips
its broken body
limp in his arms

but to no
avail.

from then onwards
everything
was sad in his life
as
he couldn't
get the sound of the falling possum
out of his
mind
until

now being aware of such things

he heard

the beautiful sound again
and turned around
just in time
to catch
another falling possum

this time saving its life

the man now understanding
why the bridge
he walked under every day
was called
suicide possum bridge.

Dannie Abse (1923–2014)

Wasp

At 3 p.m. I'm sitting in L'artista
as usual, bored, waiting for something unusual.
London's under the weather, has become prose.
Don't tell me I should be in the country
watching hypnotised animals standing
motionless in the gloom of an afternoon.

Here, at least, I'm entertained by a wasp:
it hovers near the windowsill's waxen flowers;
deluded, it dives for nectar. Afterwards in anger,
the wasp that does not know it's a wasp
becomes a little, loud, nazi insect-official.
Oblivious, in come two Jewish beards.

Next to my table, they seem to discuss Theology
– much concern about the state of a soul –
but soon, like the wasp, I twig I'm deceived
when one takes his boot off to prove his point.
Then the other remarks, 'Well, the heel's all right.'

Look! They're being served by the over-powdered,
rose-beautiful, yakking waitress. Now the wasp
decides to bully them. Who reckons a rose
is a rose is a rose? Not always, it ain't.

As for me, when I talk to myself,
I do not know whom I'm addressing.

The wasp flies to the windowpane, to its prison
So human! The door opens to the greater noise.

Alice Oswald (b. 1966)

Carol Ann Duffy (Poet Laureate 2009–19) writes: I first encountered the extraordinary work of the young poet Alice Oswald over a quarter of a century ago when I was simultaneously judging the Eric Gregory Awards and editing one of the Anvil New Poets anthologies. The former sought to encourage and the latter to introduce, but here was a poet who, modestly, only demanded awe: like coming unexpectedly upon a young deer in a forest; perfectly itself.

If we seek to recognize Truth in poetry, we must ask ourselves 'How?' Alice Oswald achieves truth through her unique word-music, a deep attentiveness to the natural world, and the marriage of both to a human feeling, or response, which almost senses itself entrapped.

The 'Listen Listen Listen Listen' here is earned by the preceding verse. 'Task/rake/ clay/mack/ black/strake' place us alongside the gardening poet as she runs for shelter in that 'summer of green rain' and we can re-live our own such epiphanies, where grasses have lifted for us and hedges have breathed as we listened. Wow.

A Greyhound in the Evening after a Long Day of Rain

Two black critical matching crows,
calling a ricochet, eating its answer,

dipped
    home

and a minute later
the ground was a wave and the sky wouldn't float.

*

With a task and a rake,
with a clay-slow boot and a yellow mack,
I bolted for shelter under the black strake dripping of timber,

summer of rain, summer of green rain
coming everywhere all day down
through a hole in my foot.

*

Listen Listen Listen Listen

*

They are returning to the rain's den,
the grey folk, rolling up their veils,
taking the steel taps out of their tips and heels.

Grass lifts, hedge breathes,
rose shakes its hair,
birds bring out all their washed songs,
puddles like long knives flash on the roads.

*

And evening is come with a late sun unloading a silence,
tiny begin-agains dancing on the night's edge.

But what I want to know is
whose is the great grey wicker-limbed hound,
like a stepping on coal, going softly away...

— ✦ —

Richard Wilbur (1921–2017)

Frank Skinner (comedian) writes: At a time when much is said about empowerment of the individual, this poem seems dangerous and counterintuitive. Its celebration of the power of yielding, the strength of acceptance, is an exhilarating challenge. I love it when a poem pulls you up short and says, stop thinking that, for a moment, and try thinking this.

Two Voices In A Meadow

A Milkweed

Anonymous as cherubs
Over the crib of God,
White seeds are floating
Out of my burst pod.
What power had I
Before I learned to yield?
Shatter me, great wind:
I shall possess the field.

A Stone

As casual as cow-dung
Under the crib of God,
I lie where chance would have me,
Up to the ears in sod.
Why should I move? To move
Befits a light desire.
The sill of Heaven would founder,
Did such as I aspire.

CHAPTER 6

'what is now will soon be past': mortality and the ticking clock

Loss is a constant. Time moves, change happens, life is short – as more than one poet declares in this section. The poems grouped here have been chosen by contributors of all ages: from tattooed teenager to great-grandmother. Not all are consoling, though even the bleakest has its own music.

The actress Lisa Dwan, a powerful performer, remembers herself as a rebellious nine-year-old changed forever by a teacher's re-enactment of Seamus Heaney's own memories of childhood loss. Adrienne Rich reminds us these transformational human connections are a key part of the poem's work; a part that the poet, far from her shadowy audience, can only imagine. Echoes and reverberation set up a kind of music between writer and reader, so even while choosing a poem that's apt for your particular, individual, distinctive loss, you are in company.

Yehuda Amichai (1924–2000)

Kate Harwood (film producer) writes: I read 'Summer or Its End' first at the beginning of an affair; that sense of being entirely present in the moment hit me then and has never left me. It's earthy, yearning, nostalgic for something that's still taking place. Recognizing even as it happens that this will one day be the past; grasping it knowingly as it starts to slip away.

Summer or Its End (extract)

Like the imprint of our bodies,
not a sign will remain that we were here.
The world closes behind us,
the sand is smoothed out again.
And already on the calendar there are dates
you will no longer exist in,
already a wind bringing clouds
that won't rain on us.

And your name is on the passenger list of
ships and in the guest books
of hotels whose very names
deaden the heart.

The three languages that I know,
all the colours that I see and dream,
won't help me.

If with a bitter mouth you speak
sweet words, the world will not grow sweet
and will not grow bitter.

And it is written in the book that we shall not fear.
And it is written that we too shall change,
like the words,
in future and in past,
in plural and loneliness.

And soon, in the coming nights,
we will appear, like wandering actors,
each in the other's dream
and in the dreams of strangers whom we didn't know
together.

—— ✎ ——

Yrsa Daley-Ward (b. 1989)

What Is Now Will Soon Be Past

Just because you do it
doesn't mean you always will.
Whether you're dancing dust
or breathing light
you're never exactly the same,
twice.

Elizabeth Parker (b. 1981)

Dry

I didn't expect you to breach the dam
loosen my banks until my clay unclenched
dropped its stash of rocks.

You sleeked my snarls of algae
brought a lush hiss to my throat
brown trout wafting their bodies.

You eased my bite
sighs of silt slid
from pebble seams.

I breathed other salts, sediments
floated light
was creamed with moon.

Then you were gone
sun stealing you
leaving me slithers, patches
where my sand tried to keep you

small darknesses tucked beneath my rocks
shrinking day by day.

— ✔ —

Sue Boyle (b. 1944)

A Leisure Centre Is Also a Temple of Learning

The honey coloured girl in the women's changing room
is absorbed in making her body more beautiful:
she has flexed and toned every muscle with a morning swim
and showered away the pool chemicals
using an aromatic scrub and a gentle exfoliant.

Lithe as a young leopard, she has perfect bone structure:
her secret cleft is shaved as neatly as a charlatan's moustache

In dreamy abstractedness she moisturises then spray perfumes
every part that might be loved. Her long hands
move in rhythm like a weaver's at a loom –
tipped throat, underchin, the little kisspoints below her ears,
the nuzzle between her breasts, her willow thighs.
She brushes her hair so clean it looks like a waterfall.

A bee could sip her.
She is summer cream slipped over raspberries.
She is so much younger than the rest of us.

She should look around.

We twelve are the chorus:

we know what happens next.

Kate Clanchy (b. 1965)

The Wedding Guest's Story

Shortly after ditching me, a matter of weeks,
in point of fact, she bought a remarkable
backless dress and got hitched to an ex-army chap
who climbs up rocks on Sundays: not the sort,

that chap, if I might explain, to stop for stragglers
or to soak up sun. He'd strike for the top
in skin tight kit, lycra shorts and pick, straining
straps around the crotch. In spite of which,

I took the half-meant invite straight, sat tight
throughout, let that dress flash a foot of flesh
to the hushed cathedral, and in my mind
I slowly climbed the low, secret steps of her spine,

swung for a while on my rope in the tuck
of her waist, scrambled sweating, swearing,
over the slopes of her shoulder blades,
to slump on the summit, weak, sobbing with loss.

— ✔ —

Rebecca Perry (b. 1986)

Dolly Alderton (journalist) writes: In my last week of flat-sharing with my best friends, this beautiful poem made me cry.

Soup Sister

And, of course,
it bothers me greatly that I can't know
the quality of the light where you are.
How your each day pans out,
how the breeze lifts the dry leaves from the street
or how the street pulls away from the rain.

Last week I passed a tree
that was exactly you in tree form,
with a kind look and tiny sub-branches
like your delicate wrists.

Six years ago we were lying
in a dark front room on perpendicular sofas,
so hungover that our skin hurt to touch.
How did we always manage to be heartbroken at the same
   time?

I could chop, de-seed and roast
a butternut squash for dinner
in the time it took you to shower.

Steam curtained the windows, whiting out
the rain, which hit the house sideways.
One of us, though I forget who, said
do you think women are treated like bowls
waiting to be filled with soup?
And the other one said, of course.

Now the world is too big,
and it's sinking and rising
and stretching out its back bones.
The rivers are too wild,
the mountains are so so old
and it's all laid out arrogantly between us.

My friend, how long do you stand
staring at the socks in your drawer
lined up neat as buns in a bakery,
losing track of time and your place in the world,
in the (custardy light of a) morning?

—— ❡ ——

Seamus Heaney (1939–2013)

Lisa Dwan (actor, director, writer, dancer) writes: I grew up in rural Ireland, and by 3rd class in National school I had figured out that the only way to overcome the awful bullying I had been subjected to was to become Top-Dog: the most outrageously behaved, fearing no consequences.

Mrs Ellis, a slight, English-accented, pale and auburn-haired woman, had returned, perhaps too prematurely, from bereavement leave. Her husband had died of a rapid cancer in September and by the time she returned in February we were feral. Mid-afternoon: we were bored and so began to make catapults with pencils and rubber bands. Wanting to impress, I took this one step too far by shooting a metal pencil sharpener into the head of a fellow student, who yelped loudly in pain.

Suddenly Mrs Ellis stepped out from behind her desk. As if in a trance she walked down the aisle towards us. She kept her face turned towards the light and summoned these words that seemed to flow through her. I did not draw breath. I could not. I was gripped in the fierce vice of her quivering voice and this spell, the marriage of her pain and this poem … 'Snowdrops/ And candles soothed the bedside …' By the time she reached the final four lines she had changed the course of my life forever.

Mid-Term Break

I sat all morning in the college sick bay
Counting bells knelling classes to a close.
At two o'clock our neighbours drove me home.

In the porch I met my father crying –
He had always taken funerals in his stride –
And Big Jim Evans saying it was a hard blow.

The baby cooed and laughed and rocked the pram
When I came in, and I was embarrassed
By old men standing up to shake my hand

And tell me they were 'sorry for my trouble'.
Whispers informed strangers I was the eldest,
Away at school, as my mother held my hand

In hers and coughed out angry tearless sighs.
At ten o'clock the ambulance arrived
With the corpse, stanched and bandaged by the nurses.

Next morning I went up into the room. Snowdrops
And candles soothed the bedside; I saw him
For the first time in six weeks. Paler now,

Wearing a poppy bruise on his left temple,
He lay in the four-foot box as in his cot.
No gaudy scars, the bumper knocked him clear.

A four-foot box, a foot for every year.

Gillian Clarke (b. 1937)

Blue Hydrangeas

You bring them in, a trug of thundercloud,
neglected in long grass and the sulk
of a wet summer. Now a weight of wet silk
in my arms like her blue dress, a load

of night-inks shaken from their hair –
her hair a flame, a shadow against light
as long ago she leaned to kiss goodnight
when downstairs was a bright elsewhere

like a lost bush of blue hydrangeas.
You found them, lovely, silky, dangerous,
their lapis lazulis, their indigoes
tide-marked and freckled with the rose

of death, beautiful in decline.
I touch my mother's skin. Touch mine.

—❧—

Simon Armitage (b. 1963)

Kate Clanchy (teacher, poet) writes: This is an early Simon Armitage work, written when the Poet Laureate was still a probation officer by day, writing poems by night under the spell of the great American poet, Frank O'Hara, and his deceptively throwaway diction.

'Any of that New York poetry that sounded like speech was exciting,' he said, in a later interview. 'I have never been able to stand that sort of writing that sounds like writing. I am much more interested when it is coming out the body and the way that people speak.' This poem opens like an O'Hara, with a series of random, even joyous images: two dishevelled young men, music on a nineties Walkman, sun on the roof, coffee with scotch.

But there's a painful truth they both know – so well they don't need to name it. It bounces back in the poem through the rhymes – Jim, anything,/Bim bom, ringing/open. Under the sunshine and rain, in the not-yet-empty wardrobe, a death.

Poem

Frank O'Hara was open on the desk
but I went straight for the directory.
Nick was out, Joey was engaged, Jim was
just making coffee and why didn't I

come over. I had Astrud Gilberto
singing 'Bim Bom' on my Sony Walkman
and the sun was drying the damp slates on
the rooftops. I walked in without ringing

and he still wasn't dressed or shaved when we
topped up the coffee with his old man's scotch
(it was only half ten but what the hell)
and took the newspapers into the porch.

Talking Heads were on the radio. I
was just about to mention the football
when he said 'Look, will you help me clear her
wardrobe out?' I said 'Sure Jim, anything.'

——— ✦ ———

Adrienne Rich (1929–2012)

Bidisha (author and broadcaster) writes: The truth of this poem
is in the connections it imagines and creates. It's a reminder of
how one crafted piece of writing, from one woman's desk, can
land in any person's hands and heart, anywhere in the world
and at any stage in a reader's life. The loose, rolling rhythm lets
us know we're in good hands, wherever we may be.

An Atlas of the Difficult World XIII (Dedications) (extract)

I know you are reading this poem
late, before leaving your office
of the one intense yellow lamp-spot and the darkening
    window

in the lassitude of a building faded to quiet
long after rush-hour. I know you are reading this poem
standing up in a bookstore far from the ocean
on a grey day of early spring, faint flakes driven
across the plains' enormous spaces around you.
I know you are reading this poem
in a room where too much has happened for you to bear
where the bedclothes lie in stagnant coils on the bed
and the open valise speaks of flight
but you cannot leave yet. I know you are reading this poem
as the underground train loses momentum and before
   running up the stairs
toward a new kind of love
your life has never allowed.
I know you are reading this poem by the light
of the television screen where soundless images jerk and
   slide
while you wait for the newscast from the *intifada*.
I know you are reading this poem in a waiting-room
of eyes met and unmeeting, of identity with strangers.
I know you are reading this poem by fluorescent light
in the boredom and fatigue of the young who are counted out,
count themselves out, at too early an age. I know
you are reading this poem through your failing sight, the thick
lens enlarging these letters beyond all meaning yet you read on
because even the alphabet is precious.
I know you are reading this poem as you pace beside the
   stove
warming milk, a crying child on your shoulder, a book in
   your hand

because life is short and you too are thirsty.
I know you are reading this poem which is not in your
    language
guessing at some words while others keep you reading
and I want to know which words they are.
I know you are reading this poem listening for something,
    torn between bitterness and hope
turning back once again to the task you cannot refuse.
I know you are reading this poem because there is nothing
    else left to read
there where you have landed, stripped as you are.

——✦——

Alan Hill (b. 1933)

Robyn Marsack (former director, Scottish Poetry Library)
writes: I love the way Alan Hill manages to be both incredulous
– none of us wishes 'to age' – and rueful in this poem. 'Dust' is
exactly right: it is associated with age, and sadly with neglect;
if you are a less than assiduous housekeeper (like me), you
tend to ignore it. Just as we tend to ignore signs of ageing:
creaky bones, wrinkles, thinning hair, forgetfulness ... Yet
they arrive, like so many truths we prefer not to acknowledge.
Hill is not sad or raging, though; rather, he is economically,
wryly observant.

That Is a Strange Day

That is a strange day
when you wake to discover
age has drifted down
imperceptibly, like dust,
and you're totally covered.

—— ◗ ——

E. E. Cummings (1894–1962)

Savannah Brown (author, model, poet, YouTube influencer) writes: This poem is essentially about how people die and even when people die, the world keeps spinning and all living things just go about their same old business. Nobody is important enough to stop the world and even after the most final and horrible and grotesque event, things and time have a way of … continuing.

I really like the last two lines (which I have tattooed on my arm) because she's buried, all's done and said, but she's by the oaks and the roses and they're going to keep growing.

It's humbling, comforting. In a thousand years all my issues with relationships or money or school or *words* or whatever won't even register as a blip on the heart monitor of the Earth. I just really like knowing that I don't matter.

when life is quite through with

when life is quite through with
and leaves say alas,
much is to do
for the swallow, that closes
a flight in the blue;

when love's had his tears out,
perhaps shall pass
a million years
(while a bee dozes
on the poppies, the dears;

when all's done and said, and
under the grass
lies her head
by oaks and roses
deliberated.)

———✦———

Christina Rossetti (1830–1894)

Joy Hunter (former typist for Winston Churchill) writes: Perhaps it's because of my age (I'm ninety-three), but I love the way this sonnet ends. Life goes on and while loved ones are deeply missed, we remember those we love for what they have given us. I would wish to be remembered for the fun and enjoyment I've had with friends and the abiding love of my four generations of family.

Remember

Remember me when I am gone away,
    Gone far away into the silent land;
    When you can no more hold me by the hand,
Nor I half turn to go yet turning stay.
Remember me when no more day by day
    You tell me of our future that you plann'd:
    Only remember me; you understand
It will be late to counsel then or pray.
Yet if you should forget me for a while
    And afterwards remember, do not grieve:
    For if the darkness and corruption leave
    A vestige of the thoughts that once I had,
Better by far you should forget and smile
    Than that you should remember and be sad.

——●——

Leo Marks (1920–2001)

Michael Morpurgo (author) writes: This is a poem full of commitment and complete affection. Poetry for me is always better spoken, for it is the music in the words that carries so much of the intensity. So when I read this, I hear it spoken by Virginia McKenna, who made it her own in the 1958 film *Carve Her Name with Pride*, about the French secret agent Violette Szabo.

The poet responsible, Leo Marks, headed the codes office supporting resistance agents in occupied Europe for the secret Special Operations Executive. At the time poems were often used to encrypt messages, but they couldn't be well-known verses, or enemy cryptanalysts would crack the code. So Marks used his own poetry.

'The Life That I Have' was composed on Christmas Eve 1943 in memory of his girlfriend Ruth, who had just died in a plane crash in Canada. On 24 March 1944, he offered the poem to Violette Szabo. She was captured, tortured and deported by the German army; she was executed, at the age of twenty-three, in Ravensbrück concentration camp in 1945.

The Life That I Have

The life that I have
Is all that I have
And the life that I have
Is yours.

The love that I have
Of the life that I have
Is yours and yours and yours.

A sleep I shall have
A rest I shall have
Yet death will be but a pause.

For the peace of my years
In the long green grass
Will be yours and yours and yours.

—— *——

Maggie Smith (b. 1977)

Good Bones

Life is short, though I keep this from my children.
Life is short, and I've shortened mine
in a thousand delicious, ill-advised ways,
a thousand deliciously ill-advised ways
I'll keep from my children. The world is at least
fifty percent terrible, and that's a conservative
estimate, though I keep this from my children.
For every bird there is a stone thrown at a bird.
For every loved child, a child broken, bagged,
sunk in a lake. Life is short and the world
is at least half terrible, and for every kind
stranger, there is one who would break you,
though I keep this from my children. I am trying
to sell them the world. Any decent realtor,
walking you through a real shithole, chirps on
about good bones: This place could be beautiful,
right? You could make this place beautiful.

CHAPTER 7

'and every mile another song': you have one life, live it

Life is not a rehearsal, better perhaps to call it a journey. While some of this chapter's poems read like traveller's tales, many more feel like celebrations of those emotions experienced while living out one's time on earth: love, lust, humour, pain, pleasure, longing.

And what riotous language this throws up! Gwyneth Lewis's 'Love Poem' slips inside the softness of a mouth, between the tongue and the teeth – no one can get closer than this. The longing of Sappho's female speaker, in Anne Carson's translation, conjures up the light steps of the woman she loves. When John Cooper Clarke's persona attempts to pin down his wife, she's always a whisker ahead, outwitting his clumsy, comical, drumbeat possessiveness just as deftly as the 'truth about love' will always elude W. H. Auden's seeker with his rat-a-tat questions.

And when the queries come too fast and thick? Maybe take the advice of Tony 'Longfella' Walsh – the hugely popular Manchester performance poet recommended here by footballer-turned-writer Marvin Sordell – and find your own particular way to eek out every last ounce of life while on that journey to the destination that awaits us all.

Kei Miller (b. 1978)

Raymond Antrobus (poet) writes: Kei Miller's poetry has always moved me with its sharp, lyrical and intelligent emotional reading of history. He understands how loaded the English language is, with pain and conquest, with brutality that is hard to forgive; he maps what James Berry and Derek Walcott have called 'the colonial hurt' with an accomplished grace and song.

This particular poem reads as a Jamaican fable or folklore, treading a line from Claude McKay's *Banana Bottom* to modern-day dub poets like Jean 'Binta' Breeze. Note the hard sounds of every ending line – 'roads', 'song', 'upon', 'done' – note the voices of the island, the prophesizing of the songs, the even/ yet uneven use of white space.

Roads

The secret roads and slaving roads,
the dirging roads, marooning roads.
   Our people sing:
   Alligator dah walk on road
   Yes, alligator dah walk on road

The cow roads and cobbled roads,
the estate roads and backbush roads.
   Our people sing:
   Go dung a Manuel Road
   Fi go bruck rock stone

The marl roads and bauxite roads
the causeway roads and Chinese roads.
　　Our people sing:
　　Right tru right tru de rocky road
　　Hear Charlie Marley call you

The press-along, the soon-be-done,
The not-an-easy, the mighty-long –
so many roads we trod upon
and every mile, another song.

———— ✦ ————

Mukahang Limbu (b. 2001)

Alice Goodman (librettist, Rector of Fulbourn, Cambridgeshire) writes: This is an immensely satisfying poem; formal, considered, sharply sensuous. It is the poem of a cultural chameleon, and as another of the species, I register the truth of the way Limbu vividly conveys taste, smell, and feeling – both emotion and touch, the hypersensitivity of arrival. I note as well how much is done through perceptions of the made world: metal and paint, the sourness of oxidation, road, car, house. And then, at the end, a hard-won resolution, as the poet moves from formality ('I know now … I did not know …I did not know') to a moment of rest ('I didn't know'). And that moment of rest is an embrace.

When I Came from Nepal

As I clutched my suitcase
thick hot sweat built up
in the slits of my palms, which
shook holding its cool
metal brace. We walked
into day-winds, thick
as dried out paint
on unwashed brown canvases.
The sky was painted daffodil yellow.
The floor was a dirty grey.
There was a metal bird:
an array of fearful,
forgotten
paint.

*

I smell the iron rust
of the Municipal Gardens.
The sour tang of home still
sits on the tip of my tongue
like the zest of sweet citrus
fizzing.

*

I did not know
of grey, gravel roads,
or the bright buzzing,
of scarlet cars.
I did not know
of lonely red-bricked houses,
gazing strangers,
standing next to next,
military officers, in endless rows.
I did not know,
of silence in the streets,
or the secret whispers on the buses,
or the sly gestures of restaurants.

In this place,
where I did not know,
the things I did not know
embrace me in ways
I didn't know.

——✦——

Liz Berry (b. 1980)

Christmas Eve

Tonight the Black Country is tinselled by sleet
falling on the little towns lit up in the darkness
like constellations – the Pigeon, the Collier –
and upon the shooting stars of boy racers
who comet through the streets in white Novas.
It's blowing in drifts from the pit banks,
over the brown ribbon of the cut, over Beacon Hill,
through the lap-loved chimneys of the factories.
Sleet is tumbling into the lap of the plastercast Mary
by the manger at St Jude's, her face gorgeous and naive
as the last Bilston carnival queen.
In the low-rise flats opposite the cemetery,
Mrs Showell is turning on her fibre-optic tree
and unfolding her ticket for the rollover lottery
though we ay never 'ad a bit o luck in ower lives
and upstairs in the box-rooms of a thousand semis
hearts are stuttering and minds unravelling
like unfinished knitting.
And the sleet fattens and softens to snow,
blanking the crowded rows of terraces
and their tiny hankies of garden, white now, surrendering
their birdfeeders and sandpits, the shed Mick built
last Autumn when the factory clammed up.
And the work's gone again
and the old boys are up at dawn to clock-on nowhere
except walk their dogs and sigh
at the cars streaming to call centres and supermarkets

because there ay nuthin in it that's mon's werk,
really bab, there ay . . .
But it's coming down now, really coming
over the stands at the Molineux, over Billy Wright
kicking his dreams into the ring road
and in the dark behind the mechanics
the O'Feeney's boy props his BMX against the lock-ups
and unzips to piss a flower into the snow
well gi'me strength, Lord, to turn the other cheek
fer we'm the only ones half way decent round ere
and the tower blocks are advent calendars,
every curtain pulled to reveal a snow-blurred face.
And it's Christmas soon, abide it or not,
for now the pubs are illuminated pink and gold
The Crooked House, Ma Pardoes, The Struggling Mon
and snow is filling women's hair like blossom
and someone is drunk already and throwing a punch
and someone is jamming a key in a changed lock
shouting *fer christ's sake, Myra, yo'll freeze me to jeth*
and a hundred new bikes are being wrapped in sheets
and small pyjamas warmed on fireguards
and children are saying *one more minute, just one, Mom*
and the old girls are watching someone die on a soap
and feeling every snow they've ever seen set in their bones.
It's snowing on us all
and I think of you, Eloise, down there in your terrace,
feeding your baby or touching his hand to the snow
and although we can't ever go back or be what we were
I can tell you, honestly, I'd give up everything I've worked for
or thought I wanted in this life,
to be with you tonight.

Edward Thomas (1878–1917)

Nicolette Jones (writer, journalist) writes: For me, this poem has always expressed, with graceful simplicity, the truth that life happens in the present. I love how Edward Thomas makes inconsequential things precious; this snippet of time when so little happens is rich and full and intense.

I love, too, the dreamy heat and stillness of summer. (Its setting echoes the two words Henry James thought the most beautiful in the English language: summer afternoon.)

It's about the fragments of the world that you see from a train – which is why I like trains. And also about looking intensely, too, like a painter might, to record a still life, to capture a scene. (My dad was a painter.) And then it's about the sense of yourself in a larger picture. It thrills me how the camera pulls out across the lovely counties while the soundtrack builds to a great chorus of birdsong.

Adlestrop

Yes. I remember Adlestrop –
The name, because one afternoon
Of heat the express-train drew up there
Unwontedly. It was late June.

The steam hissed. Someone cleared his throat.
No one left and no one came
On the bare platform. What I saw
Was Adlestrop – only the name

And willows, willow-herb, and grass,
And meadowsweet, and haycocks dry,
No whit less still and lonely fair
Than the high cloudlets in the sky.

And for that minute a blackbird sang
Close by, and round him, mistier,
Farther and farther, all the birds
Of Oxfordshire and Gloucestershire.

—— ✿ ——

Iman Mersal (b. 1966)

Mark Fiddes (poet, creative director) writes: The Egyptian poet Iman Mersal has said that poetry is 'a journey in the dark towards an unknown destination', and this is a fine example. You're aware throughout that she's trying to understand the nature of home and belonging and, therefore, identity itself.

Living and working with Arab poets, I see this theme of home and exile reoccur constantly. Here, she asks a question fundamental to the exiled: what is home for? Is it just a place to park your junk, a wall that becomes a door, or a place that stops you from falling?

Mersal also says, 'Poetry is when you are at the edge.' Many of her poems have that quality, that mild sense of vertigo. You find it here, at the top of the stairs.

The Idea of Houses

I sold my earrings at the gold store to buy a silver ring in
the market. I swapped that for old ink and a black notebook.
This was before I forgot my pages on the seat of a train
that was supposed to take me home. Whenever I arrived
in a city, it seemed my home was in a different one.

Olga says, without my having told her any of this, 'Your
home is never really home until you sell it. Then you discover
all the things you could do with the garden and the big rooms –
as if seeing it through the eyes of a broker. You've stored your
nightmares in the attic and now you have to pack them in a
suitcase or two at best.' Olga goes silent then smiles suddenly,
like a queen among her subjects, there in the kitchen between
her coffee machine and a window with a view of flowers.

Olga's husband wasn't there to witness this regal
episode. Maybe this is why he still thinks the house will
be a loyal friend when he goes blind – a house whose
foundations will hold him steady and whose stairs, out
of mercy, will protect him from falls in the dark.

I'm looking for a key that always gets lost in the bottom of
my handbag, where neither Olga nor her husband can see me
drilling myself in reality so I can give up the idea of houses.

Every time you go back home with the dirt of the world
under your nails, you stuff everything you were able to carry
with you into its closets. But you refuse to define home as

the future of junk – a place where dead things were once confused with hope. Let home be that place where you never notice the bad lighting, let it be a wall whose cracks keep growing until one day you take them for doors.

—— ✿ ——

Sappho (630 BC–570 BC)

Emily Wilson (professor of classical studies, translator of the *Odyssey*) writes: In 'Anaktoria', Sappho writes back against the monumental epic tradition, in which elite male warriors fight and kill each other for glory. The *Iliad*, created perhaps a century earlier, presents one vision of the truth about what matters in life. Sappho's poem articulates entirely different values: what is most truly beautiful might not be war, glory or courage, but the object of any individual's desire; especially the desire of women, including their desire for each other.

Sappho engages with the same mythological tradition as Homer, but suggests a new vision of Helen, the woman whose adulterous affair with Paris formed the premise for the Trojan War. Myth is tied to the female speaker's longing for her absent girlfriend. The poem traces a subtle set of associations between the massive movement of cavalry, foot soldiers and fleets, and the light steps of a woman's feet, absenting herself from one who wants her; another great truth about desire is that it's always moving, always pursuing an absence.

The original was composed to be sung to music; it is in a

regular metre, Sapphics, whose rhythm hints at skipping or dancing feet. Anne Carson's beautifully stark non-metrical translation conveys Sappho's insistence on a clear but mysterious truth.

Fragment 16

Some men say an army of horse and some men say an army
    on foot
and some men say an army of ships is the most beautiful thing
on the black earth. But I say it is
    what you love.

Easy to make this understood by all.
For she who overcame everyone
in beauty (Helen)
    left her fine husband

behind and went sailing to Troy.
Not for her children nor her dear parents
had she a thought, no—
    ]led her astray

        ]for
        ]lightly
    ]reminded me now of Anaktoria
    who is gone.

Jane Yeh (b. 1971)

A Short History of Patience

The soft chiffon of the river as it turns
Out of view. The woodpecker's stutter saying
Wish you were here. The birch branches tangled
Like wires overhead, sending mixed messages

To the birds. Baby, I could go out on a limb
And say the evening's smoky eye draws near,
The floorboards creak like a harpsichord played wrong,
The kettle rumbles with anticipation, then

Shuts itself off. Honey, without you it's cold
As a warthog's bare bottom, or the draught
That slips in under the door. Without you
I'm lonesome as a cricket in a jam jar, chirping

Till all the air runs out. *Won't you come home?*
Says the dustpan to the wandering broom.
Catch as catch can say the weeds to the scythe.
Ryegrass spreading through the yard like an open secret.
The blue line of the horizon like an eyelid, closed.

——✿——

Lorraine Mariner (b. 1974)

Kate Clanchy (poet and teacher) writes: That love is hard work, especially mother love, is a particularly unpopular truth. It doesn't often get into poems at all, and especially not into poems from the child's perspective. Yet here it is, in Lorraine Mariner's characteristic deadpan style and effortless vernacular, almost masking the workings of a Shakespearean sonnet.

I also like the setting; I spent hundreds of hours, when my children were small, standing with towels, breathing in chlorine.

Say I Forgot

Say I forgot how to love you, the way
when I was eight I forgot how to swim?
Could you steel yourself as my mother did
when she enrolled me in lessons for the holiday,
sat up in the stalls with a four-year-old
every morning for a month and afternoons
took me swimming herself in a learner pool
let me grip her hands willing me to let go?
I don't know what makes a child doubt
the water is able to keep her afloat,
think that the other side is too remote
but if I froze, could you wait it out
until I'm propelled again towards your smile
and wrapped tight in your towel like the first time?

— ✦ —

Gwyneth Lewis (b. 1959)

Love Poem

I want to be as close to you
as the name *San Juan de Aznalfarache*
when you struggle to say it. A tune in the head
you can't forget. A name
full of vitamins. A word so rich
that I catch your fillings. A rhythm,
a taste. A place
where, once, a poet was king
of Mudejar origin. *San Juan
de Aznalfarache. San
Juan de Aznalfarache*. Stumble,
stutter me before moving on
to the African citadels. Make your tongue
touch, ever so gently, the back of your teeth.
No. Let me show you. Like this.

— ✿ —

W. H. Auden (1907–1973)

O Tell Me the Truth about Love

Some say love's a little boy,
And some say it's a bird,
Some say it makes the world go round,
Some say that's absurd,
And when I asked the man next door,
Who looked as if he knew,
His wife got very cross indeed,
And said it wouldn't do.

Does it look like a pair of pyjamas,
Or the ham in a temperance hotel?
Does its odour remind one of llamas,
Or has it a comforting smell?
Is it prickly to touch as a hedge is,
Or soft as eiderdown fluff?
Is it sharp or quite smooth at the edges?
O tell me the truth about love.

Our history books refer to it
In cryptic little notes,
It's quite a common topic on
The Transatlantic boats;
I've found the subject mentioned in
Accounts of suicides,
And even seen it scribbled on
The backs of railway guides.

Does it howl like a hungry Alsatian,
Or boom like a military band?
Could one give a first-rate imitation
On a saw or a Steinway Grand?
Is its singing at parties a riot?
Does it only like Classical stuff?
Will it stop when one wants to be quiet?
O tell me the truth about love.

I looked inside the summer-house;
It wasn't even there;
I tried the Thames at Maidenhead,
And Brighton's bracing air.
I don't know what the blackbird sang,
Or what the tulip said;
But it wasn't in the chicken-run,
Or underneath the bed.

Can it pull extraordinary faces?
Is it usually sick on a swing?
Does it spend all its time at the races,
or fiddling with pieces of string?
Has it views of its own about money?
Does it think Patriotism enough?
Are its stories vulgar but funny?
O tell me the truth about love.

When it comes, will it come without warning
Just as I'm picking my nose?
Will it knock on my door in the morning,
Or tread in the bus on my toes?
Will it come like a change in the weather?
Will its greeting be courteous or rough?
Will it alter my life altogether?
O tell me the truth about love.

— ⬧ —

John Osborne (b. 1981)

There Is Handholding Still

My friend's grandparents married
three weeks after they first met.

Their third date was a pub Sunday roast,
walking her back home he proposed.

Two eighteen year olds saying
'I've got a good feeling about this.'

I think about them when I need reminding
sometimes we have to take risks.

— ⬧ —

Kim Moore (b. 1981)

If We Could Speak Like Wolves

if I could wait for weeks for the slightest change
in you, then each day hurt you in a dozen
different ways, bite heart-shaped chunks
of flesh from your thighs to test if you flinch
or if you could be trusted to endure,

if I could rub my scent along your shins to make
you mine, if a mistake could be followed
by instant retribution and end with you
rolling over to expose the stubble and grace
of your throat, if it could be forgotten

the moment the wind changed, if my eyes
could sharpen to yellow, if we journeyed
each night for miles, taking it in turns
to lead, if we could know by smell
what we are born to, if before we met

we sent our lonely howls across the estuary
where in the fading light wader birds stiffen
and take to the air, then we could agree
a role for each of us, more complicated
than alpha, more simple than marriage.

— ✦ —

Carol Ann Duffy (b. 1955)

Valentine

Not a red rose or a satin heart.

I give you an onion.
It is a moon wrapped in brown paper.
It promises light
like the careful undressing of love.

Here.
It will blind you with tears
like a lover.
It will make your reflection
a wobbling photo of grief.

I am trying to be truthful.

Not a cute card or a kissogram.

I give you an onion.
Its fierce kiss will stay on your lips,
possessive and faithful
as we are,
for as long as we are.

Take it.
Its platinum loops shrink to a wedding ring,
if you like.
Lethal.
Its scent will cling to your fingers,
cling to your knife.

John Cooper Clarke (b. 1949)

I've Fallen in Love With My Wife

The doorbell used to say ding dong
But now it bursts out into song
If I'm forlorn it ain't for long
Could I be wrong or have I
Fallen in love with my wife

Fare thee well my fairy fey
We cared so slightly anyway
Call me Krazy with a Kapital K
But I've fallen in love with my wife

I've fallen in love with my wife
She populates my days
With marital breakdown running rife
I've got to keep her under my gaze

You love somebody – set them free
That don't make no sense to me
I'm keeping her under lock and key
I've fallen in love with my wife

Rainbows and butterflies
Occupy the summer skies
Imagine my surprise
I've fallen in love with my wife

I've fallen in love with my wife
She populates my days
It's keeping me awake at night
My head stuck in this funky smaze

Every time I talk I mumble
Every time I walk I stumble
I'm dancing like a drunken uncle
I've fallen in love with my wife

I've fallen in love with my wife
She populates my days
She's not that far from a carving knife
I have to keep her in my gaze

I don't swear but what the hey
I'm all right and she's okay
Get out of our fucking way
I've fallen in love with my wife

I'm her fella she's my mate
She steals the chips right off my plate
No wonder I'm losing weight
I've fallen in love with my wife

I steal a kiss she takes the piss
We lived a life of ignorant bliss
All that and now this
I've fallen in love with my wife

Tony Walsh (b. 1965)

Marvin Sordell (footballer) writes: I have chosen this poem because, for me, it was the key that truly unlocked me as a poet and writer. 'Take This Pen' tells the reader to confidently take on the task of becoming the writer that is inside them and show the world their talent. We are all artists, with fabulous minds, yet we litter ourselves with self-doubt. 'Take This Pen' encourages us to pick up the – metaphorical – pen and begin to write our journeys. This was the poem that pushed me to write more and more. I can only thank Tony Walsh, and his poem, for the words that gave me that extra belief to follow my passion.

Take This Pen

To the kid they pick on, 'cos you're small.
The kid they kick because you're tall.
The kid they trip to watch you fall.
Poetry is *for* you. It's *for* you!

To the kid who's anxious, every day.
The last kid, when they're picked to play.
The quiet kid who has lots to say.
Poetry is *for* you.

To the kid who hides behind their hair.
Who's scared and scarred by every stare.
The kid who cries when no-one's there.
Poetry is *for* you.

To the kid that no-one sees or hears.
The kid who knows she'll end up pierced
to drain the pain of tattooed tears.
Poetry is *for* you.

To the girl who's never, ever sure
or confident, but knows she's poor.
And knows *there must be* something more.
Poetry is *for* you.

To the lad whose dad is always missed.
The kid whose mum is always pissed.
The girl with scratch marks on her wrist.
Poetry is *for* you.

To the kid not wired to follow rules.
The kid hot-wired to glow, so fools
exclude you from deluded schools and
poetry is for you.

To the kid who won't buy what we're sold.
The kid who questions what we're told.
You're a treasure chest of buried gold and
poetry is *for* you.

To the kid who feels they don't belong,
that nothing's right, that something's wrong.
But to carry weakness makes you strong so
poetry is *for* you.

To the girl whose birth was overseas
She burns and yearns to learn so she's
collecting words like a bunch of keys.
Poetry is *for* you.

To the kid who sees that reading breeds
deep feelings for his people's needs,
so he reads and reads and reads and reads.
Poetry is *for* you.

To the kid who knows that light can bring
out rainbows on a magpie's wings.
Pens song words when the songbird sings.
Poetry is *for* you.

To the kid who's never seen the sea,
but floats across the oceans, free
in dreamboats from the library.
Poetry is *for* you.

To the kid who cries for rides in cars,
but flies inside astride the stars,
finds diamond rhymes in the mines of Mars!
Poetry is *for* you.

To the kid they always call a freak,
a nerd, a wuss, a swot, a geek,
a weirdo, but you're you! Unique and
poetry is *for* you.

To that kid inside now! Fully grown.
But you still feel – somehow – on your own.
Join us. 'Cos you're not alone and
poetry is *for* you.

Welcome! We're expecting you!
We've saved a place for you. It's true
that you are us and we are you and
poetry is *for* you.

You're different. But we're the same!
Strange family, all with different names.
But we're all lit from a single flame.
And poetry is *for* you.

So here's a gift to you from me;
the pen a poet gave to me.
Take it. It will set you free.
And poetry is *for* you.

Now prick your finger, take this pen and
dip it in your blood and then you
turn your burn to nine then Zen and
poetry is *for* you.

Then lift the gift that nature gave
with graft and craft, re-draft and slave
for greatness. It awaits the brave when
poetry is *for* you.

So turn every tear you've ever wept,
and every jeer you've ever kept,
and every fear you've never slept into
poetry that's *for* you.

And think of all those stutter times,
those mutter in the gutter times.
Then put it *in* and utter lines like
poetry is *for* you.

And scribe in blood and flood the page and
stride with pride across the stage and
spit in a fit of rage that
poetry is *for* you!

And you're NOT that shy kid anymore and
THIS is what you're waiting for!
You're so much, so much, SO MUCH MORE!
And poetry is *for* you!

A giant now! No longer small!
And no-one's laughing 'cos you're tall.
From up here you can see it all!
And poetry is *for* you!

So grab the mic now, face the crowd and
tell them loud how you have vowed
to leave them wowed and how you're proud that
poetry is *for* you.

And be brilliant and unbreakable.
Distinct and unmistakable.
Unsinkable, unshakeable.
Now poetry is *for* you.

And be brave and confrontational.
Inspired and inspirational
Unafraid to be sensational!
Now poetry is *for* you.

And even if they criticize,
believe and don't apologize.
The foolish always mock the wise.
And poetry is *for* you!

But our craft outlasts their nasty games.
Their laughter only fans our flames.
And forgotten hands carve poets' names when
poetry is for you.

So we fight *because* it's frightening.
Writer's duty? Be exciting!
See the beauty! Free the lightning!
Now poetry is *for* you.

So never, ever, ever fear and
keep the flame in *here* and *here* and
shine your light and make it clear
that poetry is *for* you.

And search for more, along the way.
The lost ones that you'll find one day.
Just look into their eyes and say
that poetry is *for* you.

Then say "Here's a gift to you from me;
the pen a poet gave to me.
Take it. It will set you free.
And poetry is *for* you."

And there's easier ways to spend your days.
Huh, Jesus! Let me count the ways!
But if you … *shiver* … when a poet says
that poetry is *for* you. It's *for* you!
It's *for* you.
It's *for* you.

— ✿ —

Fleur Adcock (b. 1934)

Jenny Swann (publisher) writes: This poem is the best cure I know for insomnia. It saves me whenever I wake in the small hours and everything looks gloomy. It unfailingly makes me laugh. That final vision of all 'the worse things' – I imagine them frowning in judgement as they gather around the bed – is pure brilliance.

Things

There are worse things than having behaved foolishly in
    public.
There are worse things than these miniature betrayals,
committed or endured or suspected; there are worse things
than not being able to sleep for thinking about them.
It is 5 a.m. All the worse things come stalking in
and stand icily about the bed looking worse and worse and
    worse.

— ✦ —

Belinda Zhawi (b. 1992)

Dzoka *(Return)*

In the day,
hike this mountain
to find that place
to call home

where you can lay
your tired bones
& spread them
under the sun.

When it sets –
swallow up these nights.
With their clusters of stars,

swallow up these nights
that remind you of home
and its inky nights
around fires

   and the moon
as a woman,
with the small child on her back,
      singing…

Dzoka haungafe
　　　Dzoka haungatye
　　　　　Kufa haungafe
Kutya haungatye
　　　　Dzoka
　　　Kufa kutya
Dzoka, dzoka-a, dzoka
haungafe,
　　　　dzoka haungatye.
Kufa　　kutya – dzoka-a

In the day, hike this mountain
to find that place to call home
where you can lay your tired bones
& spread them under
　　　　　　the sun

about national poetry day

Forward Arts Foundation is the charity that co-ordinates the UK's mass participation celebration, National Poetry Day, every October. Year round, we ensure that libraries, schools and the booktrade find poets, poetry books and poetry resources, from reading lists to activity sheets, badges to bookmarks.

Our awards, the Forward Prizes, honour the best new poetry published each year: alumni include Seamus Heaney, Simon Armitage, and Claudia Rankine.

We campaign to give poetry a bigger role in public life and on the curriculum. We forge partnerships to research poetry's impact, its audiences, its reach.

As a charity, we depend on your donations to keep National Poetry Day going.

The royalties from this book support our work. Please join Cerys Matthews and all involved in this anthology in fundraising for us: there are many different ways to get involved, from sponsored memorizing of favourite poems to coffee-mornings and shared readings.

For ideas and practical details, get in touch via www.nationalpoetryday.co.uk or info@forwardartsfoundation.org

Susannah Herbert
Executive Director
Somerset House, Strand WC2A 1LR, London
2019

acknowledgements

I'd like to thank all those who made this 'people's anthology' possible, starting with the poets who have allowed me to include their poems. This anthology owes its existence to the thousands of people who responded to the call-out for poems that speak truth to them. The nominations came in all forms: pithy, long, personal, learned.

They felt like gifts: unpacking them one by one was a task tackled by Susannah Herbert of Forward Arts Foundation, with the help and support of Natalie Charles, Andrea Reece, Philippa Perry, Abi Sparrow and Tatti de Jersey. Nearer to home, Steven Abbott and Molly Mc Donald , who tickled poetry lovers I've encountered over the years enough to join in.

It's because of the affection in which National Poetry Day is held that so many poets and poetry people got behind this project, vying in generosity and selflessness to nominate poems by other poets. Will Harris, Kate Clanchy, Neil Astley, Pascale Petit, Mary Jean Chan, Mona Arshi, Vahni Capildeo, Kathleen Jamie, Imtiaz Dharker, Peter Oswald, Peter Kahn: even if the poems you nominated didn't all make it into this particular book, this time, your support has been transformational.

Suzanne Fairless Aitken tirelessly tracked down clearance and permissions. Henry Normal, whose contribution opens this book, set the tone in every way. Thanks too to Helen Taylor,

Chiggy, Nicholas Jones, William Sieghart, Kate Pakenham, A. N. Wilson. The book was born when Michael O'Mara editor Nicki Crossley first met National Poetry Day manager Andrea Reece at the 2018 London Book Fair. It fledged on Twitter and when Susannah Herbert spent afternoons on the top floor of my house, asking me why and how and what I saw in all the poems spread out before us, it finally began to sing.

The Michael O'Mara team have been wonderful to work with: thank you particularly to Nicki, but also to Gabriella Nemeth, Saskia Angenent and Lesley O'Mara.

And thanks to all my family in words, from Pippi Longstocking to Dylan Thomas, Mabinogion scribes and other 'anonymous' lost name writers, to Bob Dylan, Willie Dixon, Barrett Strong, Pauline Challacombe and Kevin Long, to Decca who let me plunder the Argo Catalogue of spoken word recordings, to Yasmin Khan for gifting me Hafiz's 'Gift', to Jeff Townes the good pied piper, to all former and future poet guests on my BBC 6 music show, Foyle Young Poets, The Poetry Society, Poet in the City, the Poetry Archive and all the wise men who can't help but try and put Humpty together again.

credits

The poems in this anthology are reprinted from the following books, all by permission of the publishers listed unless stated otherwise. Every effort has been made to trace the copyright holders of the poems published in this book. The editor and publisher apologizes if any material has been included without permission or without the appropriate acknowledgement, and would be glad to be told of anyone who has not been consulted.

Thanks are due to all the copyright holders cited below for their kind permission:

Dannie Abse, *Speak, Old Parrot* (Hutchinson, 2013) by permission of Penguin Random House UK

Fleur Adcock, *Poems 1960-2000* (Bloodaxe Books, 2000) www.bloodaxebooks.com

Yehuda Amichai, *The Selected Poetry of Yehuda Amichai*, ed. and trans. Chana Bloch & Stephen Mitchell, (University of California Press, 1996), reproduced by permission of Hana Amichai

Maya Angelou, *And Still I Rise: A Book of Poems*, copyright © 1978 by Maya Angelou. Used by permission of Random House, an imprint and division of Penguin Random House LLC. All rights reserved.

Raymond Antrobus, *The Perseverance* (Penned in the Margins, 2018)

Simon Armitage, *ZOOM!* (Bloodaxe Books, 1989) www.bloodaxebooks.com

Mona Arshi, *Small Hands* (Liverpool University Press, 2015) by kind permission of the author and publisher

Fatimah Asghar, *If They Come For Us*, copyright © 2018 by Fatimah

Asghar. Used by permission of One World, an imprint of Random House, a division of Penguin Random House LLC. All rights reserved. And also Little, Brown Book Group (Hachette)

W. H. Auden, *Collected Poems* (Random House Inc., 1976) by permission of Curtis Brown Inc.

Emily Berry, *Stranger, Baby* (Faber & Faber, 2017)

Liz Berry, *Black Country* (Chatto & Windus, 2014)

Wendell Berry, *New Collected Poems* (Counterpoint, 2012) © 2012, reprinted by permission of Counterpoint Press

Brian Bilston, *You Took the Last Bus Home* (Penguin, 2017)

Elizabeth Bishop, *The Complete Poems 1926-1979*. Copyright © 1979, 1983 by Alice Helen Methfessel. Reprinted with the permission of Farrar, Straus & Giroux, LLC.

Black, J. A., et al. *The Electronic Text Corpus of Sumerian Literature* (http://www-etcsl.orient.ox.ac.uk/), Oxford 1998-. Copyright © J.A. Black, et al. 1998, 1999, 2000, 2001. The authors have asserted their moral rights.

Sue Boyle, *Too Late for the Love Hotel* (Smith/Doorstop, 2010)

Gwendolyn Brooks, *Selected Poems* (Harper Perennial, 1963), reprinted by consent of Brooks Permissions.

C. P. Cavafy, *Collected Poems*, trans. by Edmund Keeley and Philip Sherrard. Translation copyright © 1975, 1992 by Edmund Keeley and Philip Sherrard. Reproduced with permission of Princeton University Press.

Mary Jean Chan, *Flèche* (Faber & Faber, 2019)

Kayo Chingonyi, *Kumukanda* (Chatto & Windus, 2017)

Kate Clanchy, *Slattern* (Chatto & Windus, 1995), © Kate Clanchy 1995, reproduced by permission of Rogers, Coleridge and White Ltd.

Gillian Clarke, *Ice* (Carcanet Press Ltd, 2012)

Leonard Cohen, 'Everybody Knows' by Leonard Cohen. Copyright © Leonard Cohen and Leonard Cohen Stranger Music, Inc., 1993, used by permission of The Wylie Agency (UK) Limited.

John Cooper Clarke, *The Luckiest Guy Alive* (Picador, 2019)

index of poets

— ✦ —

index of titles and first lines